AMERICAN
W·O·M·E·N

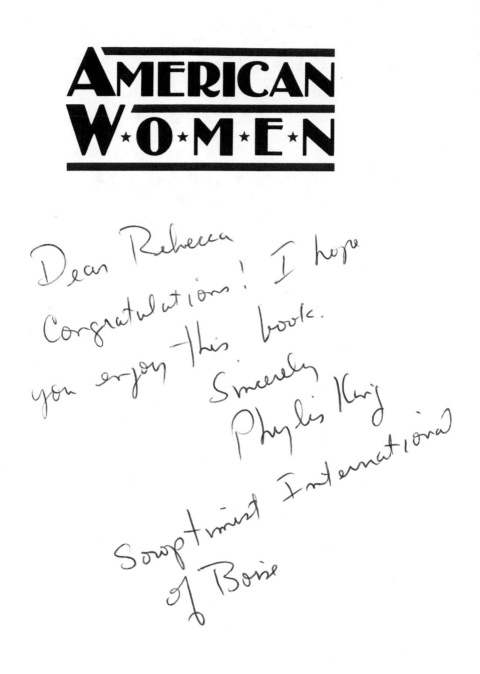

Dear Rebecca

Congratulations! I hope
you enjoy this book.
Sincerely
Phylis King

Soroptimist International
of Boise

Also by Doreen Rappaport

The Boston Coffee Party

Escape from Slavery
Five Journeys to Freedom

Living Dangerously
*American Women Who Risked Their
Lives for Adventure*

Trouble at the Mines

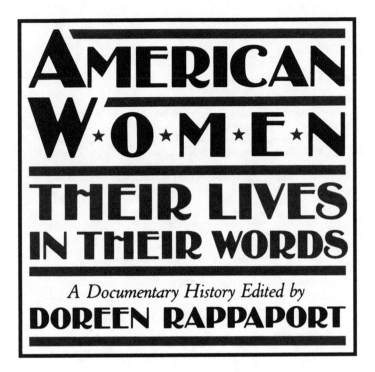

AMERICAN WOMEN

THEIR LIVES IN THEIR WORDS

A Documentary History Edited by

DOREEN RAPPAPORT

HarperCollins*Publishers*

American Women: Their Lives in Their Words
Copyright © 1990 by Doreen Rappaport
2 3 4 5 6 7 8 9 10

Library of Congress Cataloging-in-Publication Data
Rappaport, Doreen.
  American women : their lives in their words : a documentary
history / edited by Doreen Rappaport.
    p. cm.
  Includes bibliographical references.
  Summary: Excerpts from women's diaries, letters, speeches, and
autobiographical writings provide a first-person look at the history of
American women.
  ISBN 0-690-04819-X.—ISBN 0-690-04817-3 (lib. bdg.)
  1. Women—United States—History—Sources—Juvenile literature.
2. Women—United States—History—Juvenile literature.
3. Autobiography—Women authors—Juvenile literature.
[1. Women—United States—History—Sources.] I. Title.
HQ1410.R36 1990   89-77621
305.4'0973—dc20   CIP
                                                              AC
Grateful acknowledgment is made to the following for the use of photographs
in this book:
  Solomon D. Butcher Collection, Nebraska State Historical Society: 109;
Friday Associates, Inc.: 232; The Henry Francis Du Pont Winterthur
Museum: 1; Lewis W. Hine, New York Public Library Picture Collection:
161; Historic Deerfield, Inc., Deerfield, Massachusetts: 7; Kansas State
Historical Society, Topeka: 120; Dorothea Lange, Library of Congress: 215;
Library of Congress: 24, 149, 207; National Park Service, U.S. Department
of Interior: 179, 199; NASA: 275; The New York Public Library Picture
Collection: 12, 35, 42, 87, 156; Reynolds Metals Company: 240; Sears,
Roebuck Co., 1990: 203; Smith College Archives, Photograph by Katherine
E. McClellan: 93; Smithsonian Institution: 83; Union Pacific Railroad: 125;
Wyandotte County Museum, Kansas: 188.

For Susan Kempler,
for our shared commitments and vision

Acknowledgments

Every effort has been made to contact the appropriate source for material reprinted in this book. Grateful acknowledgment is made to the following for permission to reprint material:

"Fight, and If You Can't Fight, Kick": Fisk University, Special Collections

"Much Happiness": Mount Holyoke College Library Archives

"Left Our Hitherto Happy Home": The Huntington Library, San Marino, California

"There Was a Prejudice Against Female Teachers": Connecticut Historical Society

"Hogs in My Kitchen": Yale Collection of Americana, Beinecke Rare Books and Manuscript Library

"A Time Never to Be Forgotten": Chonita Lantz Earle, great-granddaughter of Maria Ascension Sepulveda y Avila

"Is Peace More a Concern of Women?": Woman's Peace Party Papers, Swarthmore College Peace Collection

"I Cannot Believe that This Is Superstitious Reverence": Wyandotte County Museum, Bonner Springs, Kansas

"A Generation Who Felt Extraordinarily Free": William Morrow and Company

"Having Learned to Stare Down Fear": Harper & Row, Publishers, Inc.

"Simply Remarkable": Oral History Collection, Columbia University. Used by permission of the trustees of Columbia University in the City of New York.

"The Problem That Has No Name": W. W. Norton & Co., Inc.

"It's in Your Own Head": *The Nation*/The Nation Company, Inc.

"Women Should Be Free to Be Anything They Want to Be": Barbara Mikulski and the American Jewish Committee

I thank Martin Fleisher, Alice Kessler-Harris, and Eli Zaretsky, who generously scrutinized the text and shared their knowledge and ideas. Arlene Hirshfelder and Beverly Singer of the Association of Indian Affairs lent their expertise to the sections on the American Indian and led me to the interview with Esther Barela. I am grateful to Chonita Lantz Earle for sharing her great-grandmother's life, and to Esther Barela, Keana Bonds, Diane Bratcher, Elda D. Cantu, Yuk Ming Liu, Daisy Rosenblum, and Angel Stimers for sharing their lives. Thelma Alston, Robb Burlage, Sharon Eubanks, John Muir, Irma Perez, Gretchen Stearns, and Lillian Moy led me to the young women who shared their lives. The following librarians and curators offered access to important material: Maida Goodwin, Smith College Archives, Beth House of Fisk University Library, George Miles of the Beinecke Rare Book and Manuscript Library, Dr. Mary Robertson of the Huntington Library, Lisa Schwarzenholz of the Wyandotte County Museum, and Everett C. Wilkie of the Connecticut Historical Society. The reference librarians at the research division of the New York Public Library led me gently through massive bibliographies and reference material. This book would not have been possible without the continued commitment and insightful criticism of my editors Barbara Fenton and Katherine Brown Tegen, the meticulous copyediting of Renée Vera Cafiero, and the assistance in picture research given by Joanna Guinther. Special thanks to Katherine Brown Tegen for her infinite patience and humor.

Contents

Author's Note

This book presents firsthand accounts of the lives of American women, from the original settlers, the Indians, to women and girls of today. An introduction for each document places the document and the woman in a historic framework. Some of the documents are produced as originally written; others have been shortened without changing their meaning. Paragraphing, punctuation, and spelling changes have been made for readability. The source of each document is found in the *Notes*, at the end of the book.

Foreword

For a long time I've wanted to create a book that would look at American history through the experiences of American women. This has long been a missing dimension in our understanding of the development of our nation. Too many books one-sidedly reconstruct history through the deeds of men, though women were active participants in shaping life in the New World even before the first European settlers arrived.

This book contains excerpts from diaries, letters, autobiographies, speeches, resolutions, essays, magazine articles, and interviews of American women. These firsthand accounts reveal the richness and variety of women's experiences and perceptions, from the first settlers, the American Indians, to today. And it reveals how the consciousness of women has changed as they have struggled with their roles in American society.

Some of these women were rebels who refused to accept society's limits on what was proper for women to do. They fought for women's equality in all areas of American life. Others led more private lives as daughters, homemakers, wives, mothers, lovers, sisters, and friends. Despite ethnic, racial, and economic differences, these women shared many common problems because they were women living in a society dominated by male authority and needs.

Some of these women were famous during their lifetimes and saw their words in print, but many never expected their words to be published. All wrote as a way of clarifying their thoughts and feelings for themselves or sharing them with close friends. Their words tell us how their world looked to them and help us see what life was like for most women in their time.

D.R.

PART ONE

WOMEN IN THE NEW WORLD

In the Beginning

For thousands of years before the first Europeans explored what is now called the United States, hundreds of groups of Indian peoples lived on the land in complex societies. Languages, customs, and cultures varied among these peoples, and so did women's lives.

In these agricultural societies, men were the hunters and warriors, women the planters, harvesters, food preparers, and givers of child care. Women gathered seeds, roots, and fruits; planted, tended, and harvested crops; butchered animals; tanned leather; wove baskets, mats, and blankets; made bowls; and rolled fiber into twine for fishing nets.

Medicine women used herbs and homemade brews

or their supernatural powers to cure their people's physical and mental problems. They received the same respect and authority as their male counterparts. Women religious leaders were called upon to use their special powers to control the weather and predict the future.

Indians told stories to explain and pass on the traditions of their cultures to the next generation. This story, from the Iroquois and Huron peoples who lived near Lake Ontario, shows the pivotal role of women in society—that women create and nurture life even at the risk of endangering their own lives.

IN THE BEGINNING there was nothing but water, a wide sea, which was peopled by various animals of the kind that live in and upon the water. It happened then that a woman fell down from the upper world. It is supposed that she was, by some mischance, pushed down by her husband through a rift in the sky. Though styled a woman, she was a divine personage.

Two loons, which were flying over the water, happened to look up and see her falling. To save her from drowning they hastened to place themselves beneath her, joining their bodies together so as to form a cushion for her to rest on. In this way they held her up, while they cried with a loud voice to summon the other animals to their aid.

The cry of the loon can be heard to a great distance, and the other creatures of the sea heard it, and assembled to learn the cause of the summons. Then came the tortoise, a mighty animal, which consented to relieve the loons of their burden. They placed the woman on the back of the tortoise, charming him to take care of her.

The tortoise then called the other animals to a grand council, to determine what should be done to preserve the life of the woman. They decided that she must have earth to live on. The tortoise directed them all to dive to the bottom of the sea and endeavor to bring up some earth. Many attempted it,—the beaver, the musk-rat, the diver, and others,—but without success. Some remained so long below that when they rose they were dead. The tortoise searched their mouths, but could find no trace of earth. At last the toad went down, and after remaining a long time rose, exhausted and nearly dead. On searching his mouth the tortoise found in it some earth, which he gave to the woman. She took it and placed it carefully around the edge of the tortoise's shell. When thus placed, it became the beginning of dry land. The land grew and extended on every side, forming at last a great country, fit for vegetation. All was sustained by the tortoise, which still supports the earth.

When the woman fell she was pregnant with twins. When these came forth they evinced opposite dispositions, the one good, the other evil. Even before they were born the same characters were manifested. They struggled together, and their mother heard them disputing. The one declared his willingness to be born in the usual manner, while the other malignantly refused, and, breaking through his mother's side, killed her. She was buried, and from her body sprang the various vegetable productions which the new earth required to fit it for the habitation of humans. From her head grew the pumpkin-vine; from her breasts the maize; from her limbs the bean.

Spooled a Piece—Milked the Cows

Francisca Hinestrosa was the first European woman after Columbus' voyages to come to the New World to live. She came with her soldier-husband on Hernando de Soto's expedition to Florida in 1539. In 1550 and 1565 other Spanish and Portuguese women settled in St. Augustine, Florida, the first permanent settlement in what is now the United States. In 1598 over a hundred women were among the four hundred Mexicans who followed the Spanish conqueror Don Juan de Onate. They established a colony in what is now known as northern New Mexico.

Seventeen Englishwomen were among the settlers who mysteriously disappeared in the colony in Roanoke, Virginia, in 1587. One hundred twenty women and children were among the 620 settlers arriving in Jamestown, Virginia, in 1609. Within twenty years Englishwomen had emigrated to Plymouth, Salem, and Boston, Massachusetts, and Dutch women to New Amsterdam and the area near what is now Albany, New York.

Bed rug made by Abigail Foote of Colchester, Connecticut

When the first women arrived in Jamestown, the single men lined up to look them over. A wife cost her passage over, 120 pounds of leaf tobacco, or about $80, a sizable sum then. The new arrivals were not forced to marry, but eventually most did.

These early arrivals fell short of the numbers needed to provide companionship for lonely male settlers, so

8

AMERICAN WOMEN

investors in the Virginia colonies started actively recruiting women from England. They signed up poor women to work as indentured servants. These women usually pledged to work for seven years in exchange for passage over and room and board.

When these volunteers did not meet the demand, women were kidnapped off the streets of English cities. Women, sentenced to long prison terms for petty or major crimes, were allowed to emigrate to the New World instead of rotting in prison or being hanged. A fourth, cheaper source of labor was introduced when the first African slaves, men and women, arrived in Jamestown.

For the first two hundred years most women in America, like most men, worked in and around the home, making almost everything the family needed. Working from well before sunup to well after sundown, women planted vegetable gardens; harvested crops; pickled and preserved vegetables and meats; milked cows; made butter and cheese; prepared meals; made soap, candles, and medicines; spun yarn; knitted scarves and stockings; and nursed sick family members. As the settlements grew and small businesses arose, women helped their husbands and sons shoe horses, cane chairs, grind eyeglasses, stitch shoes, and keep financial records. Women ran taverns, sawmills, gristmills, and dry-goods and clothing stores.

Seventeen-year-old Abigail Foote, of Colchester, Connecticut, in 1775, describes her typical day in her diary.

FIX'D GOWN FOR Prude,—Mend Mother's Riding hood—Ague in my face—Mother spun short thread—Fix'd two Gowns for Welch's girls—Carded tow—spun linen—worked on Cheese Basket—Hatchel'd Flax [separated plant fibers for spinning] with Hannah and we did 51 lb a piece—Pleated and ironed—Read a sermon of Dodridges—Spooled a piece—milked the cows—spun linen and did 50 knots—made a broom of Guinea wheat straw—Spun thread to whiten—Went to Mr. Otis's and made them a swinging visit—Israel said I might ride his jade [horse]—Set a red Dye—Prude stay'd at home and learned Eve's dream by heart—Had two scholars from Mrs Taylor's—I carded two pounds of whole wool—felt—Spun harness twine—Scoured the Pewter.

Pitty Your Destressed Daughter

One third of all colonial homes had indentured servants, and one third of these servants were women between eighteen and twenty-five. Most servants were fed just enough to keep them strong enough to work. These women were completely subject to their owners' wills. They were forbidden to leave or marry until their seven years' service were over. Whippings and punishments for minor offenses were frequent and excessive. If servants ran away and were caught, or if they became pregnant, even by their masters, their service was extended.

Elizabeth Sprigs was an indentured servant in Maryland. Her letter to her father suggests that she left England without his permission and found her new life overwhelmingly grim.

To Mr. John Sprigs White Smith
in White Cross Street near Cripple Gate London

Maryland Sept'r 22'd 1756.

Honred Father

My being for ever banished from your sight, will I hope pardon the Boldness I now take of troubling you with these, my long silence has been purely owing to my undutifullness to you, and well knowing I had offended in the highest Degree, put a tie to my tongue and pen, for fear I should be extinct from your good Graces and add a further Trouble to you, but too well knowing your care and tenderness for me so long as I retain my Duty to you, induced me once again to endeavour if possible, to kindle up that flame again.

O Dear Father, believe what I am going to relate the words of truth and sincerity, and Ballance my former bad Conduct to my sufferings here, and then I am sure you'll pitty your Destressed Daughter. What we unfortunat English People suffer here is beyond the probility of you in England to Conceive, let it suffice that I one of the unhappy Number, am toiling almost Day and Night, and very often in the

Horses druggery, and then tied up and whipp'd to that
Degree that you'd not serve an Annimal, scarce any thing
but Indian Corn and Salt to eat and that even begrudged
nay many Negroes are better used, almost naked no shoes
nor stockings to wear, and the comfort after slaving dureing
Masters pleasure, what rest we can get is to rap ourselves
up in a Blanket and ly upon the Ground, this is the deplorable
Condition your poor Betty endures, and now I beg if you
have any Bowels of Compassion left show it by sending
me some Relief, clothing is the principal thing wanting,
which if you should condiscend to, may easely send them
to me by any of the ships bound to Baltimore Town Patapsco
River Maryland, and give me leave to conclude in Duty to
you and Uncles and Aunts, and Respect to all Friends

Honred Father

Your undutifull and Disobedient Child

Elizabeth Sprigs

Please to direct for me
at Mr. Rich'd Crosses to
be left at Mr. Luxes Merc't
in Baltimore Town Patapsco River
    Maryland

Always Leap Year

As the colonies prospered in the mid-eighteenth
century, wives and daughters of wealthy farmers and
merchants were relieved of the solitary, dull, chore-
oriented life of poor women and began to enjoy the

pleasures that wealth brought. Rebecca Franks was
the daughter of a wealthy Philadelphia merchant who
was also the agent of the king of England for Pennsylvania. Franks' carefree life centered around buying and
wearing the latest fashions from England; attending
balls, concerts, and races; gossiping with friends; and
devising flirtations. She was known for her beauty,
extravagant clothes, and acid tongue.

During the Revolutionary War, Franks and her
family, like many wealthy colonists, remained loyal to
Britain. In 1780 Franks and her father visited New
York City when it was occupied by the British. In a
letter to her sister, she describes the gay social whirl
of parties, plays, and horse races in New York. Her

life is not touched by the war. Her concerns are the latest fashions, the employment of her social skills, and her ability to attract men—all crucial to capturing the right man for a good marriage, which was a woman's most important goal.

Flatbush, Saturday 10 o'clk. August 10th 1781

My Dear Abby,

By the by, few New York ladies know how to entertain company in their own houses unless they introduce the card tables except this family, (who are remarkable for their good sense and ease.) I don't know a woman or girl that can chat above half an hour, and that on the form of a cap, the colour of a ribbon or the set of a hoop-stay or jupon. I will do our ladies, that is Philadelphians, the justice to say that they have more cleverness in the turn of an eye than the New York girls have in their whole composition. With what ease, have I seen a Chew, a Penn, Oswald, Allen, and a thousand others entertain a large circle of both sexes, and the conversation without the aid of cards not flag or seem the least strain'd or stupid.

Here, you enter a room with a formal set curtsey and after the how do's, 't is a fine, or a bad day, and those trifling nothings are finish'd, all's a dead calm 'till the cards are introduced, when you see pleasure dancing in the eyes of all the matrons and they seem to gain new life. The misses, if they have a favourite swain, frequently decline playing for the pleasure of making love—for to all appearance 'tis the ladies and not the gentlemen, that shew a preference nowadays. 'Tis here, I fancy, always leap year. For my part that am used to quite another mode of behaviour, I cannot help shewing my surprise, perhaps they call it ignorance, when I see a lady single out her pet to lean almost in his arms at an Assembly or play-house, (which I give my honour I have too often seen both in married and single), and to hear a lady confess a partiality for a man who perhaps she has not seen three times. Well, I declare such a gentleman is a delightful creature, and I could love him for my husband,—or I could marry such or such a person; and scandal says most who have been married, the advances have first come from the ladie's side, or she has got a male friend to introduce him and puff her off. I fancy there wou'd be more marriage was another mode adopted; but they've made the men so saucy that I sincerely believe the lowest Ensign think 'tis but ask, and have.

Nanny Van Horn and self employed yesterday morning in trying to dress a rag baby in the fashion, but could not succeed. It shall however go, as 'twill in some degree give you an idea of the fashion as to the Jacket and pinning of the handkerchief. Yours you say reaches to the arm. I know it, but it must be pinned up to the top of the shoulder and quite under the arm, as you would a girl's Vandyke. The fuller it sets the handsomer 'tis thought. Nobody ever sets a handkerchief out in the neck,—and a gauze handkerchief is always worn double, and the largest that can be got. 'Tis pinned round the throat as Mrs. Penn always did, and made to set out before like a chitterling of a man's shirt. The ladies here always wear either a pin or broach as the men do.

Yesterday the Grenadiers had a race at the Flatlands, and in the afternoon this house swarm'd with beaux and some very smart ones. How the girls wou'd have envy'd me cou'd they have peep'd and seen how I was surrounded, and yet I shou'd have felt as happy if not much more to have spent the afternoon with the Thursday Party at the Woodlands. I am happy to hear you're out there, as the town must be dreadfull this hot summer. New York is bad enough tho' I do not think 'tis as warm as Philadelphia.

Letters this moment from you and Peggy Chew and one for Mrs Arnold—I must stop to read them. I thank you both, and let this letter for once satisfy her and you. Tell B B her apron cost a dollar, of course I have half a dollar remaining. To Nancy Coxe and all my Carolina acquaintances I beg my best love and respects. I shall as soon as I go to town this evening, send Mrs Arnold's letter. I have not seen or heard of her these two months. Her name is as little mentioned as her husband's. Mrs Robert Morris and daughters drank tea here this week. Neither of the girls are married or going to. I fancy Major B. don't wish to marry a whole family, which would be the case there. I should love to see Jem Postell—if you see him, tell him so. I don't pity Gurney. Tell Billy I oftener think of him than I fear he does of me, Mrs. Armstrong, &c. Well, this is sufficiently long—love to everybody.

Tell Peggy Chew I give her leave to read all I write if she'll take the trouble. I am happy here, tell her 'tis only for a visit—I wish to be with you.

Yours,

R. F.

I Like This Part of the World

Eliza Lucas, the daughter of a plantation owner and British military officer, lived on one of her family's plantations in South Carolina. Only six miles by water from Charles Town, Lucas enjoyed its amusements, but also shouldered unusual responsibilities for a woman. Major Lucas had sent his daughter to school in England, for he believed that the traditional American girl's education of needlework alone created "vacant and uninformed" minds. In 1739 war forced her father to return to his military post in the Caribbean. He left seventeen-year-old Eliza to run three plantations and to take care of his invalid wife.

Eliza oversaw the hired and slave help, supervised planting and harvesting, negotiated trade, kept financial records, and still found time to play the harpsichord, practice French, teach three slaves to read, keep up her correspondence, and socialize. In letters, her father encouraged her to experiment with crops other than rice. Within two years she had produced her first crop of indigo. Ten years later indigo was a southern staple.

Eliza's letter to a friend in England in 1740 reveals the delight and self-confidence of a young woman who has been given the same opportunity as men of her class to prove herself in the world.

To my good friend Mrs. Boddicott

May the 2nd

Dear Madam

I flatter myself it will be a satisfaction to you to hear I like this part of the world, as my lott has fallen here— which I really do. I prefer England to it, 'tis true, but think Carolina greatly preferable to the West Indias, and was my Papa here I should be very happy.

My Papa and Mamas great indulgence to me leave it to me to chuse our place of residence either in town or Country, but I think it more prudent as well as most agreeable to my Mama and self to be in the Country during my father's absence we are 17 mile by land and 6 by water from Charles Town where we have about 6 agreeable families around us with whom we live in great harmony.

I have a little library well furnishd for my Papa has left me most of his books in which I spend part of my time. My Musick and the Garden, which I am very fond of, take up the rest of my time that is not imployed in business, of which my father has left me a pretty good share and indeed, 'twas inavoidable as my Mama's bad state of health prevents her going through any fatigue.

I have the business of 3 plantations to transact, which requires much writing and more business and fatigue of other sorts than you can imagine. But least you should imagine it too burthensome to a girl at my early time of life, give me leave to assure you I think myself happy that I can be useful to so good a father. And by rising very early I find I can go through much business. But least you should think I shall be quite moaped with this way of life I am to inform you there is two worthy Ladies in Charles

Town, Mrs. Pinckney and Mrs. Cleland, who are partial enough to me to be always pleased to have me with them and insist upon my making their houses my home when in town and press me to relax a little much more often than tis in my honor to accept of their obliging intreaties but I sometimes am with one or the other for 3 weeks or a month at a time, and then enjoy all the pleasures Charles Town affords, but nothing gives me more than subscribing my self

Dear Madam,
Yr. most affectionet and
most obliged humble Servt.
Eliza Lucas

If Ever Two Were One

In colonial society, once a white woman married her identity was submerged in her husband's. As *femes covert* (Latin for covered or veiled women), married women were powerless. For in colonial society where property determined power, they could not buy, sell or own property, sign contracts, or draft wills. At the time of marriage, women's personal property or money became their husbands', to do with as the men wished. Women needed their husbands' approval to will their clothing or jewelry to their daughters. Married women did not even own their earnings. They had no legal identities except as their husbands' wives. In case of divorce, children were under the father's custody, not the mother's.

Widows and single women could own, buy, and sell property. They could sue and be sued and make contracts. If a husband died without a will, the widow got one third of his money and property, but she could not sell or will this property without permission from the court or the legislature. If a husband's will allowed it, a widow could administer the estate of her dead husband or relatives, will their estates to others, hold power of attorney, and be a guardian of minors.

A husband needed only to turn to the Bible to justify his wife's subordinate position. The Bible states that men were created first. Woman was created from man's rib. In biting the apple, Eve had caused the world to fall from Grace and proved that women could not resist temptation. Woman's propensity for evil needed to be restrained. As compensation and punishment for Eve's sin in Paradise, women on earth were to be helpmates, wives, and mothers. A woman belonged at home, submitting to the will of her father, brothers, and husband.

Most white women accepted society's view of their role and preferred marriage to being single. On the practical level marriage offered financial security, since single women had few opportunities to support themselves. Colonial women usually married around age twenty-one and quickly assumed their roles as homemakers and mothers. Rich or poor, they had large families. Despite miscarriages and stillbirths, and children who died in childbirth or in their early years, five to seven surviving children in one family was typical. Ten to thirteen children was not unusual.

In 1630 eighteen-year-old Anne Bradstreet immigrated to the New World with her husband and parents. Her father became deputy governor of the Massachusetts Bay Company, and her husband a company official. A dutiful wife and eventually mother of eight children, Bradstreet also wrote poems for her own pleasure and the pleasure of her family. When published, the poems brought her fame as America's first woman poet. For Bradstreet and other colonial women, a good marriage and a good family life were all-important. A good wife submitted to the will of her husband; however, a good husband treated his wife respectfully and was concerned with the needs of his family.

Bradstreet's poem "To My Dear and Loving Husband" reflects the Puritan belief that marriage is a sacred institution dedicated to the growth of love and intimacy between two people. In this excerpt from her poem "In Reference to Her Children," she explains that women gladly accept the difficulties and sacrifices of child rearing, and nurture their children so they may develop and assume their places as adults in the world. The word "dam" in this poem means mother.

To My Dear and Loving Husband

If ever two were one, then surely we.
If ever man were lov'd by wife, then thee:
If ever wife was happy in a man,
Compare with me ye women if you can.
I prize thy love more than whole Mines of gold
Or all the richest that the East doth hold.
My love is such that Rivers cannot quench,
Nor ought but love from thee, give recompence.
Thy love is such I can no way repay,
The heavens reward thee manifold I pray.
Then while we live, in love lets so persevere
That when we live no more, we may live ever.

In Reference to Her Children, 23 June 1659

I had eight birds hatch't in one nest,
Four Cocks there were, and Hens the rest.
I nursed them up with pain and care,

Nor cost, nor labour did I spare,
Till at the last they felt their wing,
Mounted the Trees, and learn'd to sing.

Great was my pain when I you bred,
Great was my care when I you fed,
Long did I keep you soft and warm,
And with my wings kept off all harm,
My cares are more and fears than ever,
My throbs such now as 'fore were never.
Alas, my birds, you wisdom want,
Of perils you are ignorant;
Oft times in grass, on trees, in flight,
Sore accidents on you may light.
O to your safety have an eye,
So happy may you live and die:

When each of you shall in your nest,
Among your young ones take your rest,
In chirping language, oft them tell,
You had a Dam that lov'd you well,
That did what could be done for young,
And nurs't you up till you were strong,
And 'fore she once would let you fly,
She shew'd you joy and misery;
Taught what was good, and what was ill,
What would save life, and what would kill.
Thus gone, amongst you I may live,
And dead, yet speak, and counsel give:
Farewel, my friends, farewel, adieu,
I happy am, if well with you.

Foul Words In My Ear

Labor shortages were a continual problem in colonial America. As news of the hard life in the New World reached Europe, the number of willing indentured servants dwindled. As small farms in the southern colonies grew into large plantations, farmers eagerly sought cheaper labor to enlarge their profits. Slave traders went to Africa and the Caribbean islands to buy able-bodied men and women to meet the growing demand for workers.

The first Africans to arrive in the New World in 1619 were indentured servants, but by 1660 black indentured servitude gave way to black slavery. Millions of Africans were taken against their will, sold by unscrupulous and greedy chieftains, or kidnapped from their homes. Separated from their families and then chained together, they were shipped to America in crowded ships with little air to breath or food to eat. Once in the New World, they were enslaved and humiliated. They were forbidden to speak their language, practice their customs, eat familiar foods, or be with their loved ones. Slavery was so entrenched in the south by the early 1770s that slaves made up two thirds of South Carolina's population and half of Virginia's.

Most slave women worked as field hands on small

A Charleston "mammy" and her charge

southern plantations. They sowed seed, picked and packed cotton, and hoed and milled corn. They were hired out to cotton and wool mills, and to tobacco plants, to earn extra money for their owners. A small number became wet nurses and house servants. In the north, slaves were household workers, farmhands, and artisans.

Slaves were property to be bought and sold at an owner's will. With no legal rights, they could not defend themselves in court or bring charges against whites. Female slaves suffered additional humiliations. Their bodies were not their own. White masters considered themselves entitled to use a female slave sexually. Her willingness was not a factor. Such sexual conquests were not thought of as rape. Children born from these sexual relations became a master's property. And because slave women were sexually pursued by their masters, they were hated and feared by their mistresses, and blamed by society for promiscuity and un-Christian morality.

In her autobiography, ex-slave Linda Brent (Harriet Jacobs) describes how the white man's sexual pursuit of slave women contaminated and shamed southern white women as well as slave women. A wedge was driven between two natural allies, both humiliated by the same person.

[IN MY FIFTEENTH YEAR] my master began to whisper foul
words in my ear. Young as I was, I could not remain
ignorant of their import. I tried to treat them with indifference
or contempt. He was a crafty man, and resorted to many
means to accomplish his purpose. He tried his utmost to
corrupt the pure principles my grandmother had instilled.
He peopled my young mind with unclean images, such as
only a vile monster could think of. I turned from him with
disgust and hatred. But he was my master. I was compelled
to live under the same roof with him. He told me I was
his property; that I must be subject to his will in all things.
My soul revolted against the mean tyranny. But where could
I turn for protection? There is no shadow of law to protect
[the slave girl] from insult, from violence, or even from
death.

My master met me at every turn, reminding me that I
belonged to him, and swearing by heaven and earth that
he would compel me to submit to him. If I went out for a
breath of fresh air, after a day of unwearied toil, his footsteps
dogged me. If I knelt by my mother's grave, his dark shadow
fell on me even there.

Mrs. Flint possessed the key to her husband's character
before I was born. She might have used this knowledge to
counsel and to screen the young and the innocent among
her slaves; but for them she had no sympathy. They were
the objects of her constant suspicion and malevolence. She
watched her husband with unceasing vigilance; but he was
well practised in means to evade it.

I had entered my sixteenth year, and every day it became
more apparent that my presence was intolerable to Mrs.

Flint. Angry words frequently passed between her and her husband. He had never punished me himself, and he would not allow any body else to punish me. In that respect, she was never satisfied; but, in her angry moods, no terms were too vile for her to bestow upon me. Yet I, whom she detested so bitterly, had far more pity for her than he had, whose duty it was to make her life happy. I never wronged her, or wished to wrong her; and one word of kindness from her would have brought me to her feet.

After repeated quarrels between the doctor and his wife, he announced his intention to take his youngest daughter, then four years old, to sleep in his apartment. It was necessary that a servant should sleep in the same room, to be on hand if the child stirred. I was selected for that office.

Mrs. Flint heard of this new arrangment, and a storm followed. I rejoiced to hear it rage.

After a while my mistress sent for me to come to her room. Her first question was, "Did you know you were to sleep in the doctor's room?"

"Yes, ma'am."

"Who told you?"

"My master."

"Will you answer all the questions I ask?"

"Yes, ma'am."

"Tell me, then, as you hope to be forgiven, are you innocent of what I have accused you?"

"I am."

She handed me a Bible, and said, "Lay your hand on your heart, kiss this holy book, and swear before God that you tell me the truth."

I took the oath she required, and I did it with a clear conscience.

"You have taken God's holy word to testify your innocence," said she. "If you have deceived me, beware! Now take this stool, sit down, look me directly in the face, and tell me all that has passed between your master and you."

I did as she ordered. As I went on with my account her color changed frequently, she wept, and sometimes groaned. She spoke in tones so sad, that I was touched by her grief. The tears came to my eyes; but I was soon convinced that her emotions arose from anger and wounded pride. She felt that her marriage vows were desecrated, her dignity insulted; but she had no compassion for the poor victim of her husband's perfidy. She pitied herself as a martyr; but she was incapable of feeling for the condition of shame and misery in which her unfortunate, helpless slave was placed.

I pitied Mrs. Flint.

Fight, and If You Can't Fight, Kick; If You Can't Kick, Then Bite

Slaves and indentured servants often resisted their oppressors. They defied their owners by sabotaging work, lying, pretending to be sick, or openly refusing to work. Their owners wrongly interpreted their resistance as laziness and stupidity. In 1781, in an unusual act of defiance, Elizabeth Freeman protested her enslavement by going to court and arguing that the Massachusetts Bill of Rights had ended slavery. She won her case and her freedom.

Sometimes resistance was violent. In 1681 a woman and two men in Massachusetts attempted to burn down their master's home. In 1741 a woman and a man tried to burn down the entire community of Charlestown, Massachusetts. Women were involved in slave revolts on Long Island in 1708, in New York City in 1712, and in Louisiana in 1732. In 1800 the Virginia militia was called out when Nancy Prosser and her husband, Gabriel, led one thousand slaves on a march into Richmond.

Cornelia (her full name is unknown) was born a slave on a small farm in Tennessee. In an interview in 1929 or 1930 Cornelia recalled her life during slavery. She speaks proudly of her mother, Fannie, an irrepressible spirit who never shied away from facing down her owners. Fannie gave her family a legacy of dignity, power, and unity despite the humiliation of enslavement.

MY MOTHER WAS the smartest black woman in Eden. She was as quick as a flash of lightning, and whatever she did could not be done better. She could do anything. She cooked, washed, ironed, spun, nursed and labored in the field. She made as good a field hand as she did a cook. I have heard Master Jennings say to his wife, "Fannie has her faults, but she can outwork any nigger in the country. I'd bet my life on that."

My mother certainly had her faults as a slave. Ma fussed, fought, and kicked all the time. I tell you, she was a demon. She said that she wouldn't be whipped, and when she fussed, all Eden must have known it. She was loud and boisterous, and it seemed to me that you could hear her a mile away. Father was often the prey of her high temper. With all her ability for work, she did not make a good slave. She was too high-spirited and independent. I tell you, she was a captain.

The one doctrine of my mother's teaching which was branded upon my senses was that I should never let anyone abuse me. "I'll kill you, gal, if you don't stand up for yourself," she would say. "Fight, and if you can't fight, kick; if you can't kick, then bite." Ma was generally willing to work, but if she didn't feel like doing something, none could make her do it. At least, the Jennings couldn't make, or didn't make her.

I was the oldest child. My mother had three other children by the time I was about six years old. It was at this age that I remember the almost daily talks of my mother on the cruelty of slavery. I would say nothing to her, but I was thinking all the time that slavery did not seem so cruel. Master and Mistress Jennings were not mean to my mother. It was she who was mean to them.

One day my mother's temper ran wild. For some reason Mistress Jennings struck her with a stick. Ma struck back and a fight followed. Mr. Jennings was not at home. For a half hour they wrestled in the kitchen. Mistress, seeing that she could not get the better of Ma, ran out into the road, with Ma right on her heels. In the road, my mother flew into her again. The thought seemed to race across my mother's mind to tear mistress' clothing off her body. She suddenly began to tear Mistress Jennings' clothes off. She caught hold, pulled, ripped and tore. Poor mistress was nearly naked when the storekeeper got to them and pulled Ma off.

"Why, Fannie, what do you mean by that?" he asked.

"Why, I'll kill her, I'll kill her dead if she ever strikes me again."

I have never been able to find out the why of the whole thing.

Pa heard Mr. Jennings say that Fannie would have to be whipped by law. He told me. Two mornings afterwards, two men came in at the big gate, one with a long lash in his hand. I was in the yard and I hoped they couldn't find Ma. To my surprise, I saw her running around the house, straight in the direction of the men. She must have seen them coming. I should have known that she wouldn't hide. She knew what they were coming for, and she intended to meet them halfway. She swooped upon them like a hawk on chickens. I believe they were afraid of her or thought she was crazy. One man had a long beard which she grabbed with one hand, and the lash with the other. Her body was made strong with madness. She was a good match for them. Mr. Jennings came and pulled her away. I don't know what would have happened if he hadn't come at that moment,

for one man had already pulled his gun out. Ma did not
see the gun until Mr. Jennings came up. On catching sight
of it, she said, "Use your gun, use it and blow my brains
out if you will."

That evening Mistress Jennings came down to the cabin.

"Well, Fannie," she said, "I'll have to send you away.
You won't be whipped, and I'm afraid you'll get killed."

"I'll go to hell or anywhere else, but I won't be whipped,"
Ma answered.

"You can't take the baby, Fannie, Aunt Mary can keep
it with the other children."

Mother said nothing at this. That night, Ma and Pa sat
up late, talking over things, I guess. Pa loved Ma, and I
heard him say, "I'm going too, Fannie." About a week
later, she told me that she and Pa were going to leave me
the next day, that they were going to Memphis. She didn't
know for how long.

"But don't be abused, Puss." She always called me Puss.
My right name was Cornelia. I cannot tell in words the
feelings I had at that time. My sorrow knew no bound.
My very soul seemed to cry out, "Gone, gone, gone forever."
I cried until my eyes looked like balls of fire. I felt for the
first time in my life that I had been abused. How cruel it
was to take my mother and father from me, I thought.
My mother had been right. Slavery was cruel, so very cruel.

Thus my mother and father were hired to Tennessee.
The next morning they were to leave. I saw Ma walking
around with the baby under her arms as if it had been a
bundle of some kind. Pa came up to the cabin with an old
mare for Ma to ride, and an old mule for himself. Mr.
Jennings was with him.

"Fannie, leave the baby with Aunt Mary," said Mr. Jennings very quietly.

At this, Ma took the baby by its feet, a foot in each hand, and with the baby's head swinging downward, she vowed to smash its brains out before she'd leave it. Tears were streaming down her face. It was seldom that Ma cried, and everyone knew that she meant every word. Ma took her baby with her.

PART TWO

THE QUESTION OF INDEPENDENCE

Nor Fitting for Your Sex

Anne Hutchinson was the first woman in America to challenge the unequal status of women. In 1634, seeking religious freedom, Hutchinson left England and settled in the Massachusetts Bay Colony. She became a respected midwife and healer in Boston. Her husband became a wealthy merchant and landowner and a highly regarded public official. Hutchinson's religious beliefs differed sharply from those of the Puritan ministers who preached that salvation was based on good deeds on earth. For Hutchinson, feeling God's grace within oneself was more important than good works. She believed that if God dwelled within a being, that person could talk directly to God. In meetings in her home, groups of up to eighty—among them important Boston merchants, landowners, and their wives—listened to her ideas. The challenge to the authority of the Puritan ministers was loud and clear.

In November 1637 and March 1638 Hutchinson was tried by both civil and religious courts for her slanderous statements. Her opponents insisted her "mixed" meetings of men and women were improper and her ideas destructive to the community's well-being. She had stepped out of the woman's proper place by daring to preach and interpret God's word as men did. Except for the Quakers, who encouraged women to be ministers, there was no European religion that recognized women's abilities and their right to assume leadership.

Hutchinson was found guilty, banished from the colony, and later excommunicated. Here is part of her trial testimony and cross-examination by John Winthrop, Governor of Massachusetts, in which she argues that she has done nothing improper before God.

[MR. WINTHROP, GOVERNOR:] Mrs. Hutchinson, you are called here as one of those that have troubled the peace of the commonwealth and the churches here. You are known to be a woman that hath had a great share in the promoting and divulging of those opinions that are causes of this trouble.

You have spoke divers things very prejudicial to the honour of the churches and ministers thereof. You have maintained a meeting and an assembly in your house that hath been condemned by the general assembly as a thing not tolerable nor comely in the sight of God nor fitting for your sex.

Therefore we have thought [it] good to send for you to understand how things are. That if you be in an erroneous way we may reduce you [so that] you may become a profitable member here among us. Otherwise if you be obstinate in your course the court may take such course that you may trouble us no further.

Why do you keep such a meeting at your house as you do every week upon a set day?

[MRS. H.:] It is lawful for me to do so, as it is all your practices. Can you find a warrant for yourself and condemn me for the same thing? When I first came to this land because I did not go to such meetings as those were, it was presently reported that I did not allow of such meetings but held them unlawful. They said I was proud and did despise all ordinances. To prevent such aspersions [I] took it up. But it was in practice before I came, therefore I was not the first.

[GOV.:] For this, that you appeal to your practice you need no confutation. If your meeting had answered to the former it had not been offensive. But I will say that there was no meeting of women alone. Your meeting is of another sort for there are sometimes men among you.

[MRS. H.:] There was never any man with us.

[GOV.:] Well, admit there was no man at your meeting and that you was sorry for it. And by what warrant do you continue such a course?

[MRS. H.:] I conceive there lyes a clear rule in Titus, that the elder women should instruct the younger and then I must have a time wherein I must do it.

[GOV.:] We find such a course as this to be greatly prejudicial to the state. Your opinions being known to be different from the word of God may seduce many simple souls that resort unto you, besides [the fact] that the occasion which hath come of late hath come from none but such as frequent your meetings, so that now they are flown off from magistrates and ministers, and this since they have come to you. [And besides the fact] that it will not well stand with the commonwealth that families should be neglected, for so many neighbours and dames and so much time spent, we see no rule of God for this. We see not that any should have authority to set up any other exercises besides what authority hath set up, and so what hurt comes of this, you will be guilty of and we for [permitting] you.

[MRS. H.:] Sir, I do not believe that to be so.

[GOV.:] Well, we see how it is we must therefore put it away from you or restrain you from maintaining this course.

[MRS. H.:] If you have a rule for it from God's word you may.

[GOV.:] We are your judges, and not you ours, and we must compel you to it.

Remember the Ladies

One hundred forty years after Anne Hutchinson's trial, nothing had changed in women's legal status. It was the beginning of the American Revolution, and the colonists were challenging the authority of the king of England and fighting for the right to make their own decisions about their lives. Though everyone understood that politics was the business of men, many women, fired by patriotism, rallied to the cause. Banding together, women refused to buy English goods until the Townshend Act of 1767, with its excessive taxes, was repealed. Women joined the "home manufacture" movement, spinning their own cloth, sewing their own clothes, and concocting home brews to replace the "illegally" taxed tea.

When war came, hundreds of women followed their husbands to battle, serving as cooks, bakers, laundresses, and nurses. The women at home kept the farms and businesses going, took care of the children, and worked for the war effort. They collected money for new recruits, sewed clothing for the army, and nursed the sick and wounded. When storekeepers tried to take advantage of the shortage of goods by selling what they had at higher prices, women organized committees to pressure merchants to set fixed prices for all goods. In Boston when a greedy merchant didn't cooperate, the women wheeled him through town, took his keys, and hoisted barrels of coffee out of his warehouse.

Abigail Adams

Abigail Adams was one of many women who managed her husband's farming and business affairs during
the war. In 1776 her husband, John, who went on to
become the second president of the United States,
was a delegate to the First Continental Congress. Like
other patriots, Abigail Adams anxiously awaited news
of the Declaration of Independence. In letters she
prodded her husband to "remember the ladies" in
the new laws. She saw the setting up of this new
government as both an opportunity to rectify the injustices of English rule and a chance to transform women's
powerlessness at the hands of their husbands as well
as their invisibility before the law.

Braintree, 31 March, 1776

I long to hear that you have declared an independency. And, by the way, in the new code of laws which I suppose it will be necessary for you to make, I desire you would remember the ladies and be more generous and favorable to them than your ancestors. Do not put such unlimited power into the hands of the husbands. Remember, all men would be tyrants if they could. If particular care and attention is not paid to the ladies, we are determined to foment a rebellion, and will not hold ourselves bound by any laws in which we have no voice or representation.

That your sex are naturally tyrannical is a truth so thoroughly established as to admit of no dispute; but such of you as wish to be happy willingly give up the harsh tide of master for the more tender and endearing one of friend. Why, then, not put it out of the power of the vicious and the lawless to use us with cruelty and indignity with impunity? Men of sense in all ages abhor those customs which treat us only as the [servants] of your sex; regard us then as being placed by Providence under your protection, and in imitation of the Supreme Being make use of that power only for our happiness.

From John Adams to Abigail Adams, April 14, 1776

As to your extraordinary code of laws, I cannot but laugh. We have been told that our struggle has loosened the bonds of government everywhere; that children and apprentices were disobedient; that schools and colleges were grown turbulent; that Indians slighted their guardians, and negroes grew insolent to their masters. But your letter was the first intimation that another tribe, more numerous and powerful than all the rest, were grown discontented. This is rather too coarse a compliment, but you are so saucy, I won't blot it out. Depend upon it, we know better than to repeal our masculine systems. Although they are in full force, you know they are little more than theory. We dare not exert our power in its full latitude. We are obliged to go fair and softly, and, in practice, you know we are the subjects. We have only the name of masters, and rather than give up this, which would completely subject us to the despotism of the petticoat, I hope General Washington and all our brave heroes would fight.

From Abigail Adams to John Adams, Braintree, 7 May 1776

I cannot say that I think you are very generous to the ladies; for, whilst you are proclaiming peace and good-will to men, emancipating all nations, you insist upon retaining an absolute power over wives. But you must remember that arbitrary power is like most other things which are very hard, very liable to be broken; and, notwithstanding all your wise laws and maxims, we have it in our power, not only to free ourselves, but to subdue our masters, and without violence, throw both your natural and legal authority at our feet.

No one remembered the ladies. The new Constitution simply ignored them. They remained without public or political power, still legally subject to their husbands.

Blacks, Native Americans, and white men who did not own property also were given no rights of citizenship.

I Would Not Go Out Unless by ye Force of a Bayonet

Grace Growden Galloway and her husband, Joseph, one of Pennsylvania's wealthiest and most important political figures, did not support the Revolution. When the war broke out, Joseph Galloway left Philadelphia and took refuge behind British lines. He returned when the British army took over Philadelphia, and he was appointed civil commissioner and superintendent of police. In June 1778, when the city fell to the patriots, Galloway and his daughter fled with the British army to New York, to leave from there for England.

Mrs. Galloway stayed behind, hoping to save the property that her father had willed to her. But as a married woman, a *feme covert*, her only legal identity was as her husband's wife. The law did not recognize her right to keep her property. The new government was empowered to take and sell property owned by Loyalists, including property to be inherited by women. Mrs. Galloway's diary for the months July–September 1778 describes her shock and growing terror over her changed social and economic position. The once carefree social visits of her women friends are now daily offerings of emotional support. When finally evicted from her home, she fears for her daughter's future, for without property her daughter has no substantial dowry with which to make a profitable marriage.

[July] Monday ye 6

I went Myself to General [Benedict] Arnold but he told Me he cou'd do Nothing in ye Case. I thought I was received rather Cooly but Civilly Sent for Mr Chew to advise with him he told Me to do Nothing but give Up everything am very low Betsay Jones is very kind

Tusday ye 7th

Molly Craig & Peggy Johns Sidnay Howell & Mrs Redman Mr Craig no men like to come to me

Tusday ye 21st

[The agents disposing of confiscated estates] took an inventory of everything even to broken China & empty bottles I left Nurse with them & call'd Sidney Howel & sat at the door with her they told Me they must advertise the house I told them they may do as they pleased but till it was decided by a Court I wou'd not go out Unless by ye force of a bayonet but when I knew who had a right to it I should know how to Act; sent for ben Chew—he came but thought I talked to high to those men; tho he himself had advised me to say all I did say but that of the force of a Bayonet in short, he Acted far from a friend & I

see plainly is rather Cold & cares little where we are brought
to beggary   he tells Me I can't stay in ye house Yet on
My saying where shou'd I go never offer'd to take Me in
no one has offer'd Me a house to shelter me   what shall
I do

Wednesday ye 22

. . . sent for Mr Dickison   he came & told Me I cou'd
Not recover dower & he fear'd my income in My estate
was forfeited likewise & [that] no tryal wou'd be of service:
but advised Me to draw up a peti'on to ye Chief Justice
Mccean for the recovery of my estate   so I find I am a
beggar   was I assured that My husband & child was happy
nothing cou'd make me very wretched

Saturday ye 25th

I am very low   every body flys from me that can assist
Me

[August] Monday ye 10th

Peggy Johns & becky Redman came in ye Morn, Lewis
sent Me word smith had gave his honour not to Molest
Me till the Opinion of ye executive council was known but
in a short time after came Peal Will & shriner with a
spanish Merchant & his attendants & took Possession of
My house   I was taken very ill & obliged to Lay down &
sent them word I cou'd not see them; they went every
Where below stairs & ye spaniard offer'd to let me chuse
My own bed chamber; but I sent them no Message   but
between 2 & 3 o'clock the last went away   Peal told Nurse

now they had given the spanish Gentle Man possession they had nothing More to do with it   but they took the Key out of ye front parlor door & locked Me out & left the windows Open; sent for Israel Pemberton & told him they had taken forcible possession of My house   he advised Me to stay in the house & take the lock of[f] ye door [and] to fasten ye window   I was fright'd & went to Gen: Arnold & told him how expos'd My house was & he kindly sent a guard   I went to bed in better spirits

Thursday ye 13th

My hopes & spirits are quite gone   they will kill me if I am Harrased Much More

Wednesday ye 19

I must go out of ye house tomorrow at 10 oclock   I was much shocked as I expected ye council had put a stop to it   am in great distress

Thursday ye 20th

after 10 oclock they Knocked Violently at the door three times   the Third Time I sent Nurse & call'd out myself to tell them I was in possession of my own House & wou'd keep so & that they should gain No admittance   Hereupon which they went round in ye yard & Try'd every door but cou'd None Open   then they went to the Kitchen door & with a scrubbing brush which they broke to pieces they forced that open   they made repeated strokes at ye door & I think it was 8 or 10 Minuets before they got it open   when then came in they look'd very Mad. I spoke first & told them I was Used ill: & show'd them the Opinion of ye Lawyers   Peel read it: peel said he had studied ye Law and knew they did right   I told them Nothing but force shou'd get me out of My house   Peel said . . . it was not ye first time he had taken a Lady by the Hand   then with the greatest air [he] said come Mrs Galloway give me your hand   I answer'd indeed I will not nor will I go out of my house but by force. he then took hold of my arm & I rose & said pray take Notice I do not leave my house of My own accord or with my own inclination but by force & Nothing but force shou'd have Made Me give up possession   Peel said with a sneer very well Madam & when he led me down ye step I said now Mr Peel let go My Arm I want not your Assistance   you Mr Peel are the last Man on earth I wou'd wish to be Obliged to

[September] Thursday ye 4th

. . . at Night I dream'd that the Vessel in which Mr G & My child sail'd in [to England] was sunk & that they were all lost   I awoke in a fright   I went to sleep again & dream'd my dear child was going home with Me to Trevose & that it rain'd & she was but poorly & by the Coachman's Not driving right we were obliged to walk to the carriage and the roads was full of water & she got wet in her feet & I was greatly distress'd but a poor fellow took her Up to Carry her to the Carriage but I was afraid she had taken her death before: we was afterward plagued about the Carriage and drove into a Narrow place & was in great danger. I awoke in great terror   What pain I feel to think My dearest child Must be drove from her Native Country & all she has taken from her & I incapable of doing any thing for her.

Woman Is to Win Every Thing
by Peace and Love

In the first half of the nineteenth century, as the industrialization of the United States began, the expanding economy offered new opportunities to earn more money and even the possibility of becoming rich. Many American men left the farms for the towns and cities. With men now working in factories, family members no longer worked side by side at home.

The world of business, trade, and government was seen as the right place for men, whom society viewed as competitive, agressive, and materialistic. Women were thought of as gentle, spiritual, and nurturing. They belonged at home, where their task was to shape future generations. Women needed male protection but men needed women's kindness and gentleness to help them hold on to spiritual values in this increasingly competitive and agressive commercial world. The idea of a woman's sphere, separate and different from the man's sphere, was accepted as an eternal truth.

Clergymen warned women to stay in their "proper place," the home, and to use their powers of persuasion there. Sarah Hale, editor of *Ladies Magazine*, the most popular women's journal of the nineteenth century, reminded her readers that home was their world.

Engraving from *Godey's Lady's Book*

From 1841 to the turn of the century, thousands of American women read Catharine Beecher's books. Beecher offered information on cooking, infant care, children's education to help women more effectively manage their homes. She praised domestic work as "the greatest work that ever was committed to human responsibility." Beecher accepted the idea of distinct spheres for women and men but insisted that within the domestic sphere, through gentle persuasion and by setting a high moral example, women could influence their husbands and sons and, through them, indirectly influence the public sphere. But she warned women that they could lose their power of gentle persuasion if they stepped out of their place.

A MAN MAY act on society by the collision of intellect, in public debate; he may urge his measures by a sense of shame, by fear and by personal interest; he may coerce by the combination of public sentiment; he may drive by physical force, and he does not outstep the boundaries of his sphere. But all the power, and all the conquests that are lawful to woman, are those only which appeal to the kindly, generous peaceful and benevolent principles.

Woman is to win every thing by peace and love; by making herself so much respected, esteemed and loved, that to yield to her opinions and to gratify her wishes, will be the free-will offering of the heart. But this is to be all accomplished in the domestic and social circle. There let every woman become so cultivated and refined in intellect, so unassuming and unambitious, so "gentle and easy to be entreated," as that every heart will repose in her presence; then, the fathers, the husbands, and the sons, will find an influence thrown around them, to which they will yield not only willingly but proudly.

But the moment woman begins to feel the promptings of ambition, or the thirst for power, her ægis of defence is gone. All the sacred protection of religion, all the generous promptings of chivalry, all the poetry of romantic gallantry, depend upon woman's retaining her place as dependent and defenceless, and making no claims, and maintaining no right but what are the gifts of honour, rectitude and love.

Whatever Is *Right* for Man to Do, Is *Right* for Woman

In the early nineteenth century many female societies sprang up, outgrowths of the religious revivals and moral reform movements of that time. Women like Catharine Beecher and Sarah Hale approved of these charitable societies as ways for women to extend influence beyond their homes, without violating their proper sphere.

Women worked as volunteers for the societies. They sold handmade clothing and knitted goods to raise money to educate male ministers, to support missionary work among Indians in the West, and to provide the less fortunate with clothes, food, and money. In cities where poverty was more widespread, women visited the poor, bringing food in one basket and religious tracts in the other. They created asylums for orphans, temporary refuges for prostitutes, and boardinghouses for working girls. The Seaman's Aid Society, headed by Sarah Hale, helped abandoned wives, widows, and children.

Women's commitment to bettering society led some to support the controversial issue of abolition. Black women and men formed their own abolition groups as early as 1826 and also joined with whites in organized groups. The First Female Anti-Slavery Society was formed in 1832 by freed black women in Salem, Massachusetts. By 1838 there were over one hundred such groups. In "ladylike" fashion, women abolitionists raised money by selling homemade goods at "antislavery fairs." They distributed antislavery literature written by men, and organized meetings where men lectured them on the evils of slavery. In not-so-ladylike fashion, they opened their homes as stations on the underground railroad for escaped slaves.

As their organizations grew, the women held national conventions, elected their own members, and planned their own campaigns. In 1837 women's societies organized a door-to-door campaign for collecting signatures to petition Congress to end slavery.

In 1836, in a bold move, the American Anti-Slavery Society had asked Angelina and Sarah Grimké, members of a wealthy South Carolina slave-owning family, to join its band of lecturers. The Grimké sisters had fled the south because they could not bear the system of slavery. Except for Quaker women ministers, only a few women had spoken in public in the two hundred years since Anne Hutchinson.

The Grimké sisters toured the north, giving firsthand accounts of the degrading lives of slaves. They emphasized that slavery corrupted whites as well as blacks. They made a special appeal to women to help their black sisters, to acknowledge the common bond that existed among all women. They urged women to use the power of petition since they did not have the power of the ballot.

At first the Grimkés spoke only to women, but private parlors proved too small for the thousands who wanted to hear them. A few ministers allowed the Grimkés to speak in their churches but insisted that only women attend the meetings. But inevitably men came to hear the sisters speak too. The Grimkés were attacked for lecturing in public to "mixed" audiences. Catharine Beecher was among the many who criticized them for stepping out of the "proper sphere" for women.

In July 1837 a "pastoral letter," written by the

Association of Congregational Ministers in Massachusetts, was read in all the Congregationalist churches
in the state. The letter, which was also published,
attacked the Grimkés, though not by name. The letter
spoke of "present dangers" that "threaten[ed] the
female character with widespread and permanent in-
jury." The ministers reminded women to perform only
their "appropriate duties and influence" as defined in
the Bible.

In a series of articles, Sarah Grimké refuted the
charges that the Bible justified women's inferior position. She insisted that God did not distinguish between
men and women as "moral and intelligent beings."
She boldly stated that the Bible was not divine in
origin. It had been written by men and reflected their
viewpoints and prejudices.

Haverhill, 7th Month 1837

Dear Friend,—

[The Pastoral Letter says,] "The appropriate duties and
influence of women are clearly stated in the New Testament.
Those duties are unobtrusive and private, but the sources
of *mighty power*. When the mild, *dependent*, softening influence
of woman upon the sternness of man's opinions is fully
exercised, society feels the effects of it in a thousand ways."
No one can desire more earnestly than I do, that woman

may move exactly in the sphere which her Creator has assigned her; and I believe her having been displaced from that sphere has introduced confusion into the world. It is, therefore, of vast importance to herself and to all the rational creation, that she should ascertain what are her duties and her privileges as a responsible and immortal being.

The New Testament has been referred to, and I am willing to abide by its decision, but must enter my protest against the false translation of some passages by the MEN who did that work, and against the perverted interpretation by the MEN who undertook to write commentaries thereon. I am inclined to think, when [women] are admitted to the honor of studying Greek and Hebrew, we shall produce some various readings of the Bible a little different from those we now have.

The Lord Jesus defines the duties of his followers in his Sermon on the Mount. He lays down grand principles by which they should be governed, without any reference to sex or condition. I follow him through all his precepts and find him giving the same directions to women as to men, never even referring to the distinction now so strenuously insisted upon between masculine and feminine virtues: this is one of the anti-christian "traditions of men" which are taught instead of the "commandments of God." Men and women were CREATED EQUAL; they are both moral and accountable beings, and whatever is *right* for man to do, is *right* for woman.

How monstrous, how anti-christian, is the doctrine that woman is to be dependent on man! Where, in all the sacred Scriptures, is this taught? Alas! she has too well learned the lesson, which MAN has labored to teach her. She has surrendered her dearest RIGHTS, and been satisfied with the privileges which man has assumed to grant her; she has been amused with the show of power, whilst man has absorbed all the reality into himself. He has adorned the creature whom God gave him as a companion, with baubles and gewgaws, turned her attention to personal attractions, offered incense to her vanity, and made her the instrument of his selfish gratification, a plaything to please his eye and amuse his hours of leisure.

This doctrine of dependence upon man is utterly at variance with the doctrine of the Bible. In that book I find nothing like the softness of woman, nor the sternness of man: both are equally commanded to bring forth the fruits of the Spirit, love, meekness, gentleness, &c. No where does God say that he made any distinction between us, as moral and intelligent beings.

All Men and Women Are Created Equal

In 1840 at the World Anti-Slavery Convention in London, women were not allowed to be seated as delegates. Lucretia Mott, a Quaker minister and founder of the Philadelphia Female Anti-Slavery Society, and Elizabeth Cady Stanton, the wife of an American abolitionist leader, were humiliated by this injustice. The two women resolved to hold a convention to "discuss the social, civil and religious rights of women" and to form a society to advocate these rights.

Eight years later, on July 14, 1848, an unsigned notice for a "women's rights convention" was placed in the *Seneca County Courier*. Despite the short notice and difficult traveling conditions, on July 19–20 over three hundred people, including forty men, attended the first women's rights meeting in Seneca Falls, New York. The women felt too insecure to chair the meeting, so Mrs. Mott's husband, James, was asked to do so and agreed.

After a number of speeches and reports on the status of women, Elizabeth Cady Stanton read the "Declaration of Rights and Sentiments," modeled on the Declaration of Independence. It listed grievances women had long suffered in a society that viewed them as inferior to men. Its resolutions demanded equal rights for women; equal access to education, business, and the professions; equality before the law and in marriage; and the right to vote. All resolutions were unanimously adopted, except the one that urged women to get the vote, for the idea of woman suffrage was considered controversial and extreme by most of the people attending the convention. One third of those present, 62 women and 38 men, signed their names to the Declaration.

The meeting attracted widespread, mostly unfavor-

REPORT

OF THE

WOMAN'S RIGHTS CONVENTION,

HELD AT

Seneca Falls, N. Y.,

JULY 19TH & 20TH, 1848.

———

ROCHESTER:
PRINTED BY JOHN DICK,
AT THE NORTH STAR OFFICE.
1848.

Cover for the report on
the first woman's rights
convention

able, press coverage. Newspaper editorials declared that women were unfit to vote. Clergymen denounced the "unwomanly" demands and untraditional behavior of all women who supported the convention. Many men and women, cowed by the ridicule and criticism, withdrew their signatures from the Declaration.

Declaration of Rights and Sentiments

WHEN, IN THE COURSE of human events, it becomes necessary for one portion of the family of man to assume among the people of the earth a position different from that which they have hitherto occupied, but one to which the laws of nature and of nature's God entitle them, a decent respect to the opinions of mankind requires that they should declare the causes that impel them to such a course.

We hold these truths to be self-evident; that all men and women are created equal; that they are endowed by their Creator with certain inalienable rights; that among these are life, liberty, and the pursuit of happiness; that to secure these rights governments are instituted, deriving their just powers from the consent of the governed. Whenever any form of government becomes destructive of these ends, it is the right of those who suffer from it to refuse allegiance to it, and to insist upon the institution of a new government, laying its foundation on such principles, and organizing its powers in such form, as to them shall seem most likely to effect their safety and happiness. Prudence, indeed, will dictate that governments long established should not be changed for light and transient causes; and accordingly all experience hath shown that mankind are more disposed to suffer, while evils are sufferable, than to right themselves by abolishing the forms to which they were accustomed. But when a long train of abuses and usurpations, pursuing invariably the same object evinces a design to reduce them under absolute despotism, it is their duty to throw off such government, and to provide new guards for their future security. Such has been the patient sufferance of the women under this government, and such is now the necessity which constrains them to demand the equal station to which they are entitled.

The history of mankind is a history of repeated injuries and usurpations on the part of man toward woman, having in direct object the establishment of an absolute tyranny over her. To prove this, let facts be submitted to a candid world.

He has never permitted her to exercise her inalienable right to the elective franchise.

He has compelled her to submit to laws, in the formation of which she had no voice.

He has withheld from her rights which are given to the most ignorant and degraded men—both natives and foreigners.

Having deprived her of this first right of a citizen, the elective franchise, thereby leaving her without representation in the halls of legislation, he has oppressed her on all sides.

He has made her, if married, in the eye of the law, civilly dead.

He has taken from her all rights in property, even to the wages she earns.

He has made her, morally, an irresponsible being, as she can commit many crimes with impunity, provided they be done in the presence of her husband. In the covenant of marriage, she is compelled to promise obedience to her husband, he becoming, to all intents and purposes, her master—the law giving him power to deprive her of her liberty, and to administer chastisement.

He has so framed the laws of divorce, as to what shall be the proper causes, and in case of separation, to whom the guardianship of the children shall be given, as to be wholly regardless of the happiness of women—the law, in all cases, going upon the false supposition of the supremacy of man, and giving all power into his hands.

After depriving her of all rights as a married woman, if

single, and the owner of property, he has taxed her to support a government which recognizes her only when her property can be made profitable to it.

He has monopolized nearly all the profitable employments, and from those she is permitted to follow, she receives but a scanty remuneration. He closes against her all the avenues to wealth and distinction which he considers most honorable to himself. As a teacher of theology, medicine, or law, she is not known.

He has denied her the facilities for obtaining a thorough education, all colleges being closed against her.

He allows her in Church, as well as State, but a subordinate position, claiming Apostolic authority for her exclusion from the ministry, and, with some exceptions, from any public participation in the affairs of the Church.

He has created a false public sentiment by giving to the world a different code of morals for men and women, by which moral delinquencies which exclude women from society, are not only tolerated, but deemed of little account in man.

He has usurped the prerogative of Jehovah himself, claiming it as his right to assign for her a sphere of action, when that belongs to her conscience and to her God.

He has endeavored, in every way that he could, to destroy her confidence in her own powers, to lessen her self-respect, and to make her willing to lead a dependent and abject life.

Now, in view of this entire disfranchisement of one-half the people of this country, their social and religious degradation—in view of the unjust laws above mentioned, and because women do feel themselves aggrieved, oppressed, and fraudulently deprived of their most sacred rights, we insist that they have immediate admission to all the rights and privileges which belong to them as citizens of the United States.

In entering upon the great work before us, we anticipate no small amount of misconception, misrepresentation, and ridicule; but we shall use every instrumentality within our power to effect our object. We shall employ agents, circulate tracts, petition the State and National legislatures, and endeavor to enlist the pulpit and the press in our behalf. We hope this Convention will be followed by a series of Conventions embracing every part of the country.

Resolutions

Resolved, That such laws as conflict, in any way, with the true and substantial happiness of woman, are contrary to the great precept of nature and of no validity, for this is "superior in obligation to any other."

Resolved, That all laws which prevent woman from occupying such a station in society as her conscience shall dictate, or which place her in a position inferior to that of man, are contrary to the great precept of nature, and therefore of no force or authority.

Resolved, That woman is man's equal—was intended to be so by the Creator, and the highest good of the race demands that she should be recognized as such.

Resolved, That the women of this country ought to be enlightened in regard to the laws under which they live, that they may no longer publish their degradation by declaring themselves satisfied with their present position, nor their ignorance, by asserting that they have all the rights they want.

Resolved, That inasmuch as man, while claiming for himself intellectual superiority, does accord to woman moral superiority, it is pre-eminently his duty to encourage her to speak and teach, as she has an opportunity, in all religious assemblies.

Resolved, That this same amount of virtue, delicacy, and refinement of behavior that is required of woman in the social state, should also be required of man, and the same transgression should be visited with equal severity in both man and woman.

Resolved, That the objection of indelicacy and impropriety, which is so often brought against woman when she addresses a public audience, comes with a very ill-grace from those who encourage, by their attendance, her appearance on the stage, in the concert, or in feats of the circus.

Resolved, That woman has too long rested satisfied in the circumscribed limits which corrupt customs and a perverted application of the scriptures have marked out for her, and that it is time she should move in the enlarged sphere which her great Creator has assigned her.

Resolved, That it is the duty of the women of this country to secure to themselves their sacred right to the elective franchise.

Resolved, That the equality of human rights results necessarily from the fact of the identity [sameness] of the race in capabilities and responsibilities.

Resolved, therefore, That, being invested by the Creator with the same capabilities, and the same consciousness of responsibility for their exercise, it is demonstrably the right and duty of woman, equally with man, to promote every righteous cause by every righteous means; and especially in regard to the great subjects of morals and religion, it is self-evidently her right to participate with her brother in teaching them, both in private and in public, by writing and by speaking, by any instrumentalities proper to be used, and in any assemblies proper to be held; and this being a self-evident truth growing out of the divinely implanted principles of human nature, any custom or authority adverse to it, whether modern or wearing the hoary sanction of antiquity, is to be regarded as a self-evident falsehood, and at war with mankind.

Resolved, That the speedy success of our cause depends upon the zealous and untiring efforts of both men and women, for the overthrow of the monopoly of the pulpit, and for the securing to woman an equal participation with men in the various trades, professions, and commerce.

And Ain't I a Woman?

The ridicule and criticism continued as women's rights conventions were held in other cities in the north and midwest. Thousands attended these conventions. Some came out of curiosity. Others came to mock and disrupt the meetings. But most women came to gather strength and feel support from the commonality of their experiences. They heard women assert their rights to equality in marriage, to divorce in unhappy unions, to the shared custody of their children, and to jobs and education. These speakers eloquently stated views that their audiences shared but were afraid to state out loud.

At the Akron, Ohio, Convention in 1851 some feminists feared that the appearance of ex-slave and abolitionist Sojourner Truth would further damage their unpopular cause. But Truth was not intimidated by their fears or by the heckling of men in the audience.

Sojourner Truth

Frances Dana Gage, who chaired the meeting, describes how Truth put the hecklers in their place and won over the audience. Truth reminded her white sisters that black women had never been put on the same pedestal with them. This speech is reproduced exactly as Gage recorded it. The dialect reflects Gage's own perception of black expression.

THE LEADERS OF the movement trembled on seeing a tall, gaunt black woman in a gray dress and white turban, surmounted with an uncouth sun-bonnet, march deliberately into the church, walk with the air of a queen up the aisle, and take her seat upon the pulpit steps. A buzz of disapprobation was heard all over the house, and there fell on the listening ear, "An abolition affair!" "Woman's rights and niggers!" "I told you so!" "Go it, darkey!"

At my request order was restored, and the business of the Convention went on. Morning, afternoon, and evening exercises came and went. Through all these sessions old Sojourner, quiet and reticent, sat crouched against the wall on the corner of the pulpit stairs, her sun-bonnet shading her eyes, her elbows on her knees, her chin resting on her broad, hard palms. At intermission she was busy selling the "Life of Sojourner Truth," a narrative of her own strange and adventurous life. Again and again, timorous and trembling ones came to me and said, with earnestness, "Don't let her speak, Mrs. Gage, it will ruin us. Every newspaper in the land will have our cause mixed up with abolition and niggers, and we shall be utterly denounced." My only answer was, "We shall see when the time comes."

There were very few women in those days who dared to "speak in meeting"; and the august teachers of the people [ministers] were seemingly getting the better of us, while the boys in the galleries, and the sneerers among the pews, were hugely enjoying the discomfiture, as they supposed, of the "strong-minded." Some of the tender-skinned friends were on the point of losing dignity, and the atmosphere betokened a storm. When, slowly from her seat in the corner rose Sojourner Truth, who, till now, had scarcely lifted her head. "Don't let her speak!" gasped half a dozen in my ear. She moved slowly and solemnly to the front, laid her old bonnet at her feet, and turned her great speaking eyes to me. There was a hissing sound of dissapprobation above and below. I rose and announced "Sojourner Truth," and begged the audience to keep silence a few moments.

The tumult subsided at once, and every eye was fixed on this almost Amazon form, which stood nearly six feet high, head erect, and eyes piercing the upper air like one in a dream. At her first word there was a profound hush. She spoke in deep tones, which, though not loud, reached every ear in the house, and away through the throng at the doors and windows.

"Wall, chilern, whar dar is so much racket dar must be somethin' out of kilter. I tink dat 'twixt de niggers of de Souf and de womin at de Norf, all talkin' 'bout rights, de white men will be in a fix pretty soon. But what's all dis here talkin' 'bout?

"Dat man ober there say dat womin needs to be helped into carriages, and lifted ober ditches, and to hab de best place everywhar. Nobody eber helps me into carriages, or ober mud-puddles, or gibs me any best place!" And raising herself to her full height, and her voice to a pitch like rolling thunder, she asked, "And a'n't I a woman? Look at me! Look at my arm! (and she bared her right arm to the shoulder, showing her tremendous muscular power). I have ploughed, and planted, and gathered into barns, and no man could head me. And a'n't I a woman? I could work as much and eat as much as a man—when I could get it—and bear de lash as well! And a'n't I a woman? I have born thirteen children, and seen 'em mos' all sold off to slavery, and when I cried out with my mother's grief, none but Jesus heard me! And a'n't I a woman?

"Den dey talks 'bout dis ting in de head; what dis dey call it?" ("Intellect," whispered some one near.) "Dat's it, honey. What's dat got to do wid womin's rights or niggers' rights? If my cup won't hold but a pint, and yours holds a quart, wouldn't ye be mean not to let me have my little half-measure full?" And she pointed her significant [index] finger, and sent a keen glance at the minister who had made the argument. The cheering was long and loud.

"Den dat little man in black dar [a minister], he say women can't have as much rights as men, 'cause Christ wan't a woman! Whar did your Christ come from?" Rolling thunder couldn't have stilled that crowd, as did those deep, wonderful tones, as she stood there with outstretched arms and eyes of fire. Raising her voice still louder, she repeated, "Whar did your Christ come from? From God and a woman! Man had nothin' to do wid Him."

Turning again to another objector, she took up the defense of Mother Eve. "If de fust woman God ever made was strong enough to turn the world upside down all alone, dese women togedder (and she glanced her eye over the platform) ought to be able to turn it back, and get it right side up again! And now dey is asking to do it, de men better let 'em." Long-continued cheering greeted this. "Bleeged to ye for hearin' on me, and now ole Sojourner han't got nothin' more to say."

Amid roars of applause, she returned to her corner, leaving more than one of us with streaming eyes, and hearts beating with gratitude. She had taken us up in her strong arms and carried us safely over the slough of difficulty turning the whole tide in our favor. I have never in my life seen anything like the magical influence that subdued the snobbish spirit of the day and turned the sneers and jeers of an excited crowd into notes of respect and admiration.

While Acknowledging Our Mutual Affection . . .

By 1848, the time of the first woman's rights convention in Seneca Falls, the status of married women had changed little since colonial times. They still had no control over their earnings and property and no rights to guardianship of their children. Mississippi was the first state to pass a married Women's Property Law, in 1839. In 1848, after a thirteen-year petition campaign, New York State lawmakers gave women control over their property and wages but refused to give them the right to sell or will property or money. By 1850 most states had passed laws giving married women the right to own property. The motivation behind these laws was not necessarily to help women but to protect large property owners who wanted to leave their holdings to their female children who would pass these holdings onto their male descendants.

The inequality of married women to married men before the law, and the inequality within most marriages, had convinced Lucy Stone that her life plans couldn't include marriage to a master. Stone met Henry Blackwell, a successful businessman and ardent abolitionist, while on a lecture tour for women's rights. He courted Stone for two years despite her declaration that she would never marry.

Gradually Blackwell won Stone's respect and love. He agreed that theirs would be a marriage of equality. The word "obey" was taken out of the traditional marriage vows, and their vows read, "Do you take this man to be your lawfully wedded husband, to love and honor till death do you part?" At Blackwell's suggestion, they read a protest against the marriage laws at their wedding ceremony in 1855. The protest was later published and widely circulated. After marriage, Stone kept her own last name, and other women who also chose to do so were dubbed "Lucy Stoners."

WHILE ACKNOWLEDGING OUR mutual respect by publicly assuming the relationship of husband and wife, yet in justice to ourselves and a great principle, we deem it a duty to declare that this act on our part implies no sanction of, nor promise of voluntary obedience to such of the present laws of marriage, as refuse to recognize the wife as an independent, rational being, while they confer upon the husband an injurious and unnatural superiority, investing him with legal powers which no honorable man would exercise, and which no man should possess.

We believe that personal independence and equal human rights can never be forfeited, except for crime; that marriage should be an equal and permanent partnership, and so recognized by law; that until it is recognized, married partners should provide against the radical injustice of present laws, by every means in their power.

We believe that where domestic difficulties arise, no appeal should be made to legal tribunals under existing laws, but that all difficulties should be submitted to the equitable adjustment of arbitrators mutually chosen.

Thus reverencing law, we enter our protest against rules and customs which are unworthy of the name, since they violate justice, the essence of the law.

Our Arrival Set a Buzz Going

When the Civil War broke out in 1861, women again played a vitally important part in helping the war effort. As in the Revolutionary War, in addition

to their normal work, women often did the work of absent husbands, brothers, or fathers. Northern and Southern women organized local aid societies. They sewed and knitted clothing, shipped food and medicine, and helped families whose men were in battle. In the North, the U.S. Sanitary Commission, created largely by women, supervised hospitals, recruited nurses, and set up convalescent homes.

Northern abolitionists continued to speak up for their brothers and sisters in chains. Elizabeth Cady Stanton and Susan B. Anthony organized the National Women's Loyal League, which collected over 400,000 signatures petitioning Congress for an amendment to end slavery.

When the war ended in 1865, Congress passed the Thirteenth Amendment, forbidding slavery. Abolitionists set out to get the vote for the newly freed blacks. The suffragists expected that their male allies in the abolitionist movement would campaign for women to get the vote, too. But most male abolitionists felt that black men needed their freedom guaranteed before women achieved equality, and that pressing for woman suffrage might destroy the chance for black male suffrage.

In 1866 the suffragists formed the American Equal Rights Association to seek the vote for freedmen and all women. A year later Kansas became their first test, when its citizens were asked to decide whether black men and/or women should be allowed to vote. Much to the suffragists' dismay, they found that most blacks in Kansas were not supporting woman suffrage, feeling that the "woman question" would hurt their chance for the vote.

Lucy Stone and Susan B. Anthony reported their vigorous stomp through Kansas to Elizabeth Cady Stanton, who by this time had produced many controversial writings on women's rights, divorce, the Bible and suffrage. As a mother of seven, Stanton did not feel able to leave her children behind and travel with the frequency necessary for political organizing. In fact,

she was usually so busy and harried fulfilling her domestic duties that Susan B. Anthony, who remained single, often baby-sat for Stanton in order to free her to write her speeches. Stanton's problem, of combining motherhood with her career as a political activist and writer, plagued other nineteenth-century women as well, for society expected that women alone were responsible for child care. This problem persists into our own times.

D. R. Anthony's House, Leavenworth
April 11, 1867

Dear Mrs. Stanton:

Our arrival set a buzz going, and when I announced you and Susan and Aunt Fanny for the fall, they began to say "they guessed the thing would carry."

I fully expect we shall carry the State. But it will be necessary to have a good force here in the fall, and you will have to come. Our meetings are everywhere crowded to overflowing, and in every case the papers speak well of them. We have meetings for every night till the 4th of May. By that time we shall be well tired out. The women here are grand. One woman in Wyandotte said she carried petitions all through the town for female suffrage, and not one woman in ten refused to sign. Another in Lawrence said they sent up two large petitions from there. So they have been at the Legislature, like the heroes they really are, and it is not possible for the husbands of such women to back out, though they have sad lack of principle and a terrible desire for office.

Yours, [*Lucy Stone*]

Apparently the opponents of woman suffrage were maneuvering to confine the issue to race and avoid a vote on the issue of sex, as Lucy Stone explains in this letter.

Atchison, May 9, 1867

Just now there is a plot to get the Republican party to drop the word "male," and also to agree to canvass *only* for the word "white." There is a call, signed by the Chairman of the State Central Republican Committee, to meet at Topeka on the 15th, to pledge the party to the canvass on that single issue. As soon as we saw the call and the change of tone of some of the papers, we sent letters to all those whom we had found true to principle, urging them to be at Topeka and vote for both words. This effort of ours the Central Committee know nothing of, and we hope they will be defeated, as they will be sure to be surprised. So, till this action of the Republicans is settled, we can affirm nothing. Everywhere we go we have the largest and most enthusiastic meetings, and any one of our audiences would give a majority for woman suffrage. But the negros are all against us.

Lucy Stone

P.S.—The papers here are coming down on us, and every prominent reformer, and charging us with being Free Lovers.

A newspaper correspondent covered a debate between a Kansas judge and Olympia Brown, the first ordained woman minister in the United States, who spent July through October in Kansas campaigning for woman suffrage:

Judge Sears [who spoke in favor of Manhood Suffrage] made really a fine speech. It was expected that when Miss Brown was introduced many would leave, owing to the strange feelings against Female Suffrage in and about Oscaloosa; but not one left, the crowd grew more dense. A more eloquent speech never was uttered in this town than Miss Brown delivered; for an hour and three-quarters the audience was spell-bound as she took up each point advanced by her opponent, not denying their truth, but showing by unanswerable logic that if it were good under certain reasons for the negro to vote, it was ten times better for the same reasons for the women to vote.

She said the ballot meant protection; it means much more; it means education, progress, advancement, elevation for the oppressed classes, drawing a glowing comparison between the working classes of England and those of the United States. She scorned the idea of an aristocracy based upon two accidents of the body. She paid an eloquent tribute to Kansas, the pioneer in all reforms, and said that it would be the best advertisement that Kansas could have to give the ballot to women, for thousands now waiting and uncertain, would flock to our State, and a vast tide of emigration would continually roll toward Kansas until her broad and fertile prairies would be peopled. It is useless to attempt to report her address, as she could hardly find a place to stop. When she had done, her opponent had nothing to say, he had been beaten on his own ground, and retired with his feathers drooping. After Miss Brown had closed, some one in the audience called for a vote on the female proposition. The vote was put, and nearly every man and woman in the house rose simultaneously, men that had fought the proposition from the first arose, even Judge Sears himself looked as though he would like to rise, but his principles, much tempted, forbade. After the first vote, Judge Sears called for a vote on his, the negro proposition, when about one-half the house arose.

Salina, Kansas, Sept. 12, 1867

Dear Friend:

To-day we go to Ellsworth, the very last trading post on the frontier. A car load of wounded soldiers went East on the train this morning; but the fight was a few miles West of Ellsworth. No Indians venture to that point.

Our tracts gave out at Solomon, and the Topeka people failed to fill my telegraphic order to send package here. Our tracts do more than half the battle; reading matter is so very scarce that everybody clutches at a book of any kind.

Send 2,000 of Curtis' speeches, 2,000 of Phillips', 2,000 of Beecher's, and 1,000 of each of the others, and then fill the boxes with the reports of our last convention; they are the best in the main because they have everybody's speeches together.

[*Susan B. Anthony*]

Their energetic campaign did not work: the men in Kansas denied the vote to women as well as to black men. While the suffragists campaigned in Kansas, they also lobbied Congress to delete the word "male" from the proposed Fourteenth Amendment, which would forbid the states to deny the vote to "male citizens" over twenty-one. In a national petition campaign women asked lawmakers not to pass any amendment that disenfranchised citizens on the grounds of sex. But woman suffrage supporters in Congress were the minority.

In 1868, when the Fourteenth Amendment passed, the word "male" was still in it. In February 1869, Congress passed the Fifteenth Amendment. It guaranteed that a citizen's right to vote could not be denied or abridged on the grounds of race, color, or having once been a slave. Quarrels developed among the suffragists over whether or not to help in the ratification campaign. The Equal Rights Association supported the amendment, but Elizabeth Cady Stanton and Susan B. Anthony didn't. They formed a new group—the National Woman Suffrage Association (NWSA). The opposition formed the American Woman Suffrage Association (AWSA). In the next twenty years, despite vociferous state-by-state campaigning, the women won the vote in only four states. The fight for woman suffrage had just begun.

PART THREE

SEEKING AN EDUCATION

Puddings and Seams

Like Abigail Adams, Judith Sargent Murray believed that the revolutionary statement in the Declaration of Independence that "all men are created equal" included women, and that women were also endowed with certain natural and unalienable rights. Murray was the daughter of a wealthy shipowner and merchant in Gloucester, Massachusetts. As a young child she was so bright that her parents let her sit in on her brother's tutorials for entrance to Harvard. What did she feel when she realized that despite her intellectual gifts, higher education was closed to her solely because she was a woman?

Sometime during the Revolution Murray wrote an

essay, "On the Equality of the Sexes," in which she
rejected the idea that men were intellectually superior
to women. She argued that intellectual differences between the two sexes were due to differences of educational opportunities.

IS IT UPON mature consideration we adopt the idea, that
nature is thus partial in her distributions? Is it indeed a
fact, that she hath yielded to one half of the human species
so questionable a mental superiority? From what doth this
superiority [of men] proceed[?] May we not trace its source
in the difference of education, and continued advantages?
Will it be said that the judgment of a male two years old,
is more sage than that of a female of the same age? I
believe the reverse is generally observed to be true. But
from that period what partiality! how is the one exalted
and the other depressed, by the contrary modes of education
which are adopted! the one is taught to aspire, the other
is early confined and limited. As their years increase, the
sister must be wholly domesticated, while the brother is
led by the hand through all the flowery paths of science.

At length arrived at womanhood, the uncultivated fair
one feels a void, which the employments allotted her are
by no means capable of filling. What can she do? To books,
she may not apply; or if she doth, *to those only of the novel
kind*, lest she merit the appelation of a *learned lady*; and
what ideas have been affixed to this term, the observation
of many can testify. Meantime she herself is most unhappy;
she feels the want of a cultivated mind. Is she single, she
in vain seeks to fill up time from sexual employments or

Women's activities were confined to the home

amusements. Is she united to a person whose soul nature made equal to her own, education hath set him so far above her, that in those entertainments which are productive of such rational felicity, she is not qualified to accompany him. She experiences a mortifying consciousness of inferiority, which embitters every enjoyment. Doth [her husband] possess a mind incapable of improvement, she is equally wretched, in being so closely connected with an individual whom she cannot but despise.

Now, was she permitted the same instructors as her brother for the employment of a rational mind an ample field would be opened. In astronomy she might catch a glimpse of the immensity of the Deity, and thence she would form amazing conceptions of the august and supreme Intelligence. In geography she would admire Jehovah in the midst of his benevolence; thus adapting this globe to the various wants and amusements of its inhabitants. In natural philosophy she would adore the infinite majesty of heaven, clothed in condescension; and as she traversed the reptile world, she would hail the goodness of a creating God. A mind, thus filled, would have little room for the trifles with which our sex are, with too much justice, accused of amusing themselves, and they would thus be rendered fit companions for those, who should one day wear them as their crown.

I would calmly ask, is it reasonable, that a candidate for immortality, for the joys of heaven, an intelligent being, who is to spend an eternity in contemplating the works of Diety, should at present be so degraded, as to be allowed no other ideas, than those which are suggested by the mechanism of a pudding, or the sewing of the seams of a garment?

Promise Not to Tell

Very few white colonial women had even the limited educational opportunities of Judith Sargent Murray. In the 1700s no more than half the white women in America could write a proper letter, or even sign their names. After the Revolution the belief that the new nation needed better-educated citizens led to more public schools for boys. By 1800 white girls attended primary schools with boys.

Black girls seeking an education faced the double problem of racism and sexism. In the eighteenth century most northern common schools barred free blacks. In 1774 the Quakers set up schools for black children in Pennsylvania. Catherine Ferguson, a slave who bought her freedom, opened a school in New York City in 1793 for poor blacks and whites. When Sarah Mapps Douglass, a free black, opened a school for blacks in Philadelphia in 1820, there were already nine other such private schools in the city. In 1853 Douglass went to teach at the Institute for Colored Youth, a Quaker-sponsored school which trained black women as teachers.

A few northern whites opened their schools to blacks. In 1833 Prudence Crandall accepted a black student in her Connecticut Academy. For the next year and a half townspeople vandalized the school and stoned pupils and teachers. No one would sell Crandall food and supplies. She closed the school after an arsonist gutted the cellar and masked men swung battering rams at the school walls. In 1851 Myrtilla Miner opened a teacher training school for black girls in Washington, D.C. Mrs. Miner kept the school going for eight years despite harassment and violence.

In the south, after the slave rebellions of 1800,

1822, and 1831, laws were passed forbidding the teaching of reading to slaves. A few sympathetic whites taught slaves to read, but most learning came from an educational underground, planned by blacks for blacks. And in most cases it was black women who led these secret crusades for literacy. In her autobiography Susie King Taylor describes her early schooling.

I WAS BORN under the slave law in Georgia in 1848 and was brought up by my grandmother in Savannah. There were three of us with her, my younger sister and brother. My brother and I being the two eldest, we were sent to a friend of my grandmother, Mrs. Woodhouse, a widow, to learn to read and write. She was a free woman and lived on Bay Lane, between Habersham and Price Streets, about half a mile from my house. We went every day with our books wrapped in paper to prevent the police or white persons from seeing them. We went in, one at a time, through the gate into the yard to the kitchen, which was the school room. She had 25 or 30 children whom she taught, assisted by her daughter, Mary Jane. The neighbors would see us going in some time, but they supposed we were there learning trades, as it was the custom to give children a trade of some kind. After school, we left the same way we entered, one by one and we would go to a square about a block from the school and wait for each other. I remained at her school for two years or more, when I was sent to a Mrs. Mary Beasley, where I continued until May 1860, when she told my grandmother she had taught me all she knew, and grandmother had better get someone else who could teach me more, so I stopped my studies for a while.

I had a white playmate about this time, named Katie O'Connor, who lived on the next corner of the street from my house and who attended a convent. One day she told me, if I would promise not to tell her father, she would give me some lessons. On my promise not to do so, and gaining her mother's consent, she gave me lessons about four months every evening. At the end of this time she was put into the convent permanently, and I've never seen her since.

A month after this James Blouis, our landlord's son, was attending the high school and was very fond of grandmother, so she asked him to give me a few lessons which he did until the middle of 1861, when the Savannah Volunteer Guards, to which he and his brother belonged were ordered to the front.

Much Happiness

In the early 1800s, as more white girls attended primary school, female literacy rose, but higher education for women existed only for the well-to-do. At female academies young women learned embroidery, painting, singing, French, and harpsichord. The new democracy saw no reason for women to learn Latin, Greek, history, or science. There was no practical need for such knowledge when women's lives centered around their families.

But some women had different beliefs about women's entitlement to education. In 1819 Emma Willard, a teacher at a girls' academy, asked the New York state legislature to fund an institution of higher learning for women. (Willard did not give her speech personally before the male lawmakers, as they would have considered it improper.)

Willard's speech was carefully constructed so that nothing in it would threaten the traditional view of women. She assured the legislators that her school would be "as different from those appropriate to the other sex, as the female character and duties are for the male." Her curriculum would produce better homemakers and better teachers. Teaching was a suitable occupation for women, who were by nature nurturers and molders of children, and willing to work for even less pay than men. When the legislature refused to fund her school, Willard raised the money from citizens in Troy. In 1821 the Troy Female Seminary opened and eventually became a model training school for teachers.

Mary Lyons, a teacher at another female academy, also wanted to establish an endowed school of higher learning for women. Lyons wanted to provide "a solid, extensive, and well-balanced English education [to] prepare ladies to be *educators* of children and youth,

rather than to fit them to be mere teachers." Lyons
also insisted that married women needed a "well-
balanced education to guide their families."

In 1837, after four grueling years of fundraising,
Mary Lyons opened the Mount Holyoke Female Seminary in South Hadley, Massachusetts, which is now
Mount Holyoke College. Its three-year curriculum
covered many subjects studied by college men: grammar, ancient and modern geography, ancient and modern history, algebra, human physiology, botany, natural
and intellectual philosophy, as well as calisthenics, mu-
sic, and French. To cut down on the costs of running
the school, students were required to perform domestic
chores—cooking, serving, cleaning.

Smith College students practicing basketball

Antoinette Hubbell wrote a friend about a typical day.

AT PRESENT I study half an hour before breakfast, from $5\frac{1}{2}$ till 6. From $\frac{1}{4}7$ to $7\frac{1}{4}$ is one of my precious half hours for secret retirement. At $7\frac{1}{2}$ I join one of the classes for calisthenics, 15 min. At $\frac{1}{4}8$ we meet in the Seminary Hall for family devotions. Immediately after leaving the hall I go out for exercise in the open air. The remainder of the forenoon is occupied with study and recitation.

We dine at 12, after which I spend the time until $1\frac{1}{2}$ on French. We are translating one of Racine's tragedies, Esther. I study Latin for the succeeding day till 2. Between 2 & 3 Mon. and Thurs. sing, with a choir of 25 or 30, while most of the others are drawing. Tues. I am employed that hour folding sheets and table cloths, with one other, Miss Charlotte Hyde.

At 3 we assemble for sectional exercises, 15 min. At $3\frac{1}{4}$ Miss Lyon meets us all in the hall, taking for herself half an hour to instruct us [on] various subjects: today, (Tues.) she has just finished that of health, upon the various branches of which she has spoken for several weeks past. We then go to our rooms to study $\frac{3}{4}$ of an hour till $4\frac{1}{2}$. I spend it analyzing, parsing, etc., [or] preparing my chemistry or Latin. The remaining $\frac{3}{4}$ of an hour till the bell rings for the close of study hours at $5\frac{1}{4}$ is passed Mon. and Thurs. in the grammar class.

The interval till tea time, at 6, is variously employed in social intercourse, sewing, writing, procuring wood and water for our rooms, etc. At 7 the bell rings for study. From $7\frac{1}{2}$

to 8 secret devotion,—recess, 15 minutes, then mental exercise again until the retiring bell at $9\frac{1}{4}$. Truly I think we demonstrate the possibility of putting the motto "Early to bed and early to rise" in practice.

You will see two reasons why we are so contented here. We are constantly employed; (and oh, how much happiness, right kinds of employment impart:) there is also much variety with great regularity in our engagements which always gives interest.

Works by the Piece

In the 1830s, while a few privileged women were attending college, many unmarried farm women, for whom a college education was not an economic possibility, went to work in textile mills. With the spinning jenny and power loom in wide use, factory life became a reality in the northeast of the United States. Mill owners in Lowell, Massachusetts, and other towns, in need of a reliable, cheap labor, turned to women. The advertisements for good wages, cheery factories, and boardinghouses surrounded by neat lawns reassured parents that their daughters would have more than suitable living and working accommodations. The knowledge that their daughters would also be properly supervised, have strict curfews, and attend church regularly further bolstered the image of Lowell's high moral standards.

The young women were eager to leave home. Here was their chance to be independent, to earn their own money, and to be with other like-minded young women. They considered mill work temporary work, a stopgap before marriage. The new recruits enjoyed the companionship of other women and the experience of being on their own. They enjoyed the debating clubs, where they discussed topics of current interest. They read books and magazines from the lending library, and their own writings were published in the company magazine, *Lowell Offering*.

But the women soon realized that life in Lowell was not an educational experience, and that claims of this sort were essentially hypocritical. Their working and living conditions were less than ideal. They slept six in a room, three to a bed. The curfews of ten P.M. were too strict. Not attending church on Sunday was grounds for being fired. Despite the facade of cheery factory buildings, the insides of the mills were cramped and filled with foul air. Work was monotonous. Twelve-hour days were exhausting. Wages were low. Pay was deducted if a worker was late to work, or if the overseer thought the work completed was poor. If orders were not obeyed, the worker was immediately fired. Speed-ups and unexpected wage cuts happened whenever owners felt business slipping.

In defense, the women banded together to better

their miserable working conditions and low pay, and to offset the overwhelming power of their employers. In February 1834 when wages were cut in Lowell, the women went on strike. In 1836 when boarding fees were raised without wages also being raised, the women walked off their jobs again. The strikes failed, but organizing continued. By May 1845 the Lowell Female Labor Reform Association, headed by weaver Sarah G. Bagley, had 600 members.

Shoemakers' strike in Lynn, Massachusetts

In 1845 workers from Lowell, Fall River, and Andover petitioned the state legislature for a ten-hour-day law. Out of the 2,139 petition signatures, 1,151 were from Lowell. On February 13, 1845, six women workers and three men testified at the first governmental investigation into labor conditions. The employers also testified. Then the committee went to Lowell for a firsthand look. They left "fully satisfied" that nothing at the mills could be improved. The lawmakers did not recommend a ten-hour day.

Here is Eliza R. Hemmingway's testimony about working conditions in Lowell.

THE FIRST PETITIONER who testified was Eliza R. Hemmingway. She had worked 2 years and 9 months in the Lowell Factories; 2 years in the Middlesex, and 9 months in the Hamilton Corporations. Her employment is weaving—works by the piece. The Hamilton Mill manufactures cotton fabrics. The Middlesex, woollen fabrics. She is now at work in the Middlesex Mills, and attends one loom. Her wages average from $16 to $23 a month exclusive of board. She complained of the hours for labor being too many, and the time for meals too limited. In the summer season, the work is commenced at 5 o'clock, A.M., and continued until 7 o'clock, P.M., with half an hour for breakfast and three quarters of an hour for dinner. During eight months of the year, but half an hour is allowed for dinner. The air in the room she considered not to be wholesome. There were 293 small lamps and 61 large lamps lighted in the room in which she worked, when evening work is required. These lamps are also lighted sometimes in the morning. About 130 females, 11 men, and 12 children (between the ages of 11 and 14) work in the room with her.

She thought the children enjoyed about as good health as children generally do. The children work but 9 months out of 12. The other 3 months they must attend school. Thinks that there is no day when there are less than six of the females out of the mill from sickness. There was more sickness in the Summer than in Winter months; though in the Summer, lamps are not lighted. She thought there was a general desire among the females to work but ten hours, regardless of pay. Most of the girls are from the country, who work in the Lowell Mills. The average time which they remain there is about three years. She knew one girl who had worked there 14 years. Her health was poor when she left. Miss Hemmingway said her health was better where she now worked, than it was when she worked on the Hamilton Corporation.

She knew of one girl who last winter went into the mill at half past 4 o'clock, A.M. and worked till half past 7 o'clock, P.M. She did so to make more money. She earned from $25 to $30 per month. There is always a large number of girls at the gate wishing to get in before the bell rings. They do this to make more wages. A large number come to Lowell to make money to aid their parents who are poor. She knew of many cases where married women came to Lowell and worked in the mills to assist their husbands to pay for their farms. The moral character of the operatives is good. There was only one American female in the room with her who could not write her name.

A Most Extraordinary Case

Women were recruited for the low-paying, dangerous, and dull jobs in the textile mills, but they were
excluded from the professions. By the time of the
first women's rights convention in 1848, only the low-
paying profession of teaching was open to women.
The fields of medicine, law, politics, theology, and
science were closed. Small numbers of women published
their own newspapers, wrote books, and ran successful
businesses, but these ventures were independent and
did not usually require formal education or licensing
by authorities. Some women took over the family business when their father died and their brothers were
elsewhere. Dissatisfied with the limited horizons for
their lives, some nineteenth-century women risked re-
jection, humiliation, and loneliness and set out to enter
the professions.

In 1843, while teaching school, Elizabeth Blackwell
became determined to become a doctor, despite the
fact that no medical school accepted women. She continued teaching to support herself, studying medicine
with two sympathetic doctors after work. She applied
to twenty-nine medical schools before she was accepted
in 1847 at Geneva College, a small school in rural
upstate New York. Blackwell later learned that the

students, asked by the administration to decide whether or not to admit a woman, thought the request was a joke, and joined in the joke by accepting her. In her autobiography Blackwell describes her first days in medical school.

I HAD NOT the slightest idea of the commotion created by my appearance as a medical student in the little town. Very slowly I perceived that a doctor's wife at the table avoided any communication with me, and that as I walked backwards and forwards to college the ladies stopped to stare at me, as at a curious animal. I afterwards found that I had so shocked Geneva propriety that the theory was fully established either that I was a bad woman, whose designs would gradually become evident, or that, being insane, an outbreak of insanity would soon be apparent. Feeling the unfriendliness of the people, though quite unaware of all this gossip, I never walked abroad, but hastening daily to my college as a sure refuge, I knew when I shut the great doors behind me that I shut out all unkindly criticisms, and I soon felt perfectly at home amongst my fellow-students.

The following extracts from my journal of those days show how any early difficulties were successfully overcome:

November 9.—My first happy day; I feel really encouraged. The little fat Professor of Anatomy is a capital fellow; certainly I shall love fat men more than lean ones henceforth. He will afford me every advantage, and says I shall graduate with éclat. Then, too, I am glad that they like the notoriety of the thing, and think it a good "spec."

November 10.—Attended the demonstrator's evening lecture—very clear—how superior to books! Oh, this is the way to learn! The class behaves very well; and people all seem to grow kind.

November 15.—To-day, a second operation at which I was not allowed to be present. This annoys me. I was quite saddened and discouraged by Dr. Webster requesting me to be absent from some of his demonstrations. I don't believe it is his wish. I wrote to him hoping to change things.

November 17.—Dr. Webster seemed much pleased with my note, and quite cheered me by his wish to read it to the class to-morrow, saying if they were all actuated by such sentiments the medical class at Geneva would be a very noble one. He could hardly guess how much I needed a little praise. I have no fear of the kind students.

November 22.—A trying day, and I feel almost worn out, though it was encouraging too, and in some measure a triumph; but 'tis a terrible ordeal! That dissection was just as much as I could bear. Some of the students blushed, some were hysterical, not one could keep in a smile, and some who I am sure would not hurt my feelings for the world if it depended on them, held down their faces and shook. My delicacy was certainly shocked, and yet the exhibition was in some sense ludicrous. I had to pinch my hand till the blood nearly came, and call on Christ to help me from smiling, for that would have ruined everything; but I sat in grave indifference, though the effort made my heart palpitate most painfully. Dr. Webster, who had perhaps the most trying position, behaved admirably.

November 24.—To-day the Doctor read my note to the class. In this note I told him that I was there as a student with an earnest purpose, and as a student simply I should be regarded; that the study of anatomy was a most serious one, exciting profound reference, and the suggestion to absent myself from any lectures seemed to me a grave mistake. I did not wish to do so, but would yield to any wish of the class without hesitation, if it was their desire. I stayed in the ante-room whilst the note was being read. I listened joyfully to the very hearty approbation with which it was received by the class, and then entered the amphitheatre and quietly resumed my place. The Doctor told me he felt quite relieved.

No further difficulty ever afterwards occurred.

The behavior of the medical class during the two years that I was with them was admirable.

In 1849, upon graduation, Blackwell became the first woman doctor in the United States. In 1851 she went to New York City to set up a medical practice. Hospitals refused to let her patients in. Landlords refused to rent her an office. Other doctors shunned her.

THE FIRST SEVEN years of New York life were years of very difficult, though steady, uphill work. Patients came very slowly to consult me. I had no medical companionship, the profession stood aloof, and society was distrustful of the innovation. Insolent letters occasionally came by post, and my pecuniary position was a source of constant anxiety.

My first medical consultation was a curious experience. In a severe case of pneumonia in an elderly lady I called in consultation a kind-hearted physician of high standing who had been present in Cincinnati at the time of my father's fatal illness. This gentleman, after seeing the patient, went with me into the parlour. There he began to walk about the room in some agitation, exclaiming, "A most extraordinary case! Such a one never happened to me before; I really do not know what to do!" I listened in surprise and much perplexity, as it was a clear case of pneumonia and of no unusual degree of danger, until at last I discovered that his perplexity related to *me*, not to the patient, and to the propriety of consulting with a lady physician! I was both amused and relieved. I at once assured my old acquaintance that it need not be considered in the light of an ordinary consultation, if he were uneasy about it, but as a friendly talk. So, finally, he gave me his best advice; my patient rapidly got well, and happily I never afterwards had any difficulty in obtaining a necessary consultation from members of the profession.

Although I have never met with any serious difficulties in attending to my practice at all hours of the night, yet unpleasant annoyances from unprincipled men were not infrequent. Some well-dressed man would walk by my side on Broadway, saying in a low voice, "Turn down Duane Street to the right"; or whilst waiting for a horse-car at midnight by the City Hall a policeman would try to take my hand; or a group of late revellers would shout across the street, "See that lone woman walking like mad!" But with common sense, self-reliance, and attention to the work at hand, any woman can pursue the medical calling without risk.

These malicious [remarks] are painful to me, for I am

woman as well as physician, and both natures are wounded by these falsehoods. Ah, I am glad I, and not another, have to bear this pioneer work. I understand why this life has never been lived before. It *is* hard, with no support but a high purpose, to live against every species of social opposition. I *should* like a little fun now and then. Life is altogether too sober.

By 1857 Blackwell had raised enough money to buy a building and open the New York Infirmary for Women and Children. The hospital was staffed by Elizabeth Blackwell, her sister, Dr. Emily Blackwell, and Dr. Marie E. Zakrzewska. Nine years later she opened the Women's Medical College of New York Infirmary, the first medical school for women.

All Sorts of Excuses

For most Southern black girls, receiving an education was impossible until after the Civil War. As part of Reconstruction, Northern teachers were appointed to the Freedmen's Bureau to educate the former slaves. Despite their awareness that they were an unwanted presence among white Southerners and that living conditions would be hard, over seven thousand teachers, mostly black and white women, went south. In addition to teaching reading and writing, the women ran Sunday schools, tended the sick, sewed clothes for newborns, buried those who didn't survive, and comforted their families.

Getting a college education was more difficult for Southern blacks. Paying the tuition for the newly established black colleges such as Howard, Fisk, and Hampton Institute was a terrible struggle for most students. Many studied for a semester, and then taught until they earned the next semester's expenses, alternating teaching and college until they finished their education. Graduates of the Freedmen's Schools and the black colleges went on to become teachers of future generations of blacks.

Chinese Americans, like black Americans, were considered inferior to whites, and barred from public education. In 1859, after years of petitioning by the Chinese to get their children into San Francisco's schools, the Board of Education reluctantly allowed the Chinese into evening classes for foreigners and opened a day school for Chinese children.

But by the late 1860s anti-Chinese feeling closed the school and barred the Chinese from evening schools. Chinese children went to church-sponsored day schools, and working adults attended evening classes in churches.

In 1884 Mary and Joseph Tape went to enroll

their daughter Mamie in their neighborhood school. When admission was refused, the Tapes went to court. They argued that Mamie, as a natural-born citizen, was entitled to the same free education as other natural-born citizens. The county judge agreed and so did the California Supreme Court, but the school board refused to budge.

On April 7, 1885, Mamie's lawyer took her to the neighborhood school. The principal refused her admission on the technicalities that Mamie didn't have a vaccination certificate and that class size already exceeded the limit set by the school board. The principal agreed to put Mamie on the waiting list.

The next day Mrs. Tape wrote a letter to the school board expressing her anger and anguish.

1769 Green Street
San Francisco, April 8, 1885

To the Board of Education—Dear Sirs: I see that you are going to make all sorts of excuses to keep my child out of the Public Schools. Dear sirs, Will you please tell me! Is it a disgrace to be born a Chinese? Didn't God make us all!!! What right! have you to bar my child out of the school because she is a chinese Descend. They is no other worldly reason that you could keep her out, except that I suppose, you all goes to churches on Sundays! Do you call that a Christian act to compell my little children to go so far to a school that is made in purpose for them.

If I had any wish to send [my child] to a chinese school I could have sent them two years ago without going to all this trouble. You have expended a lot of Public money foolishly, all because of one poor little Child.

Her playmates is all Caucasians ever since she could toddle around. If she is good enough to play with them! Then is she not good enough to be in the same room and studie with them? You had better come and see for yourselves. See if the Tape's is not same as other Caucasians, except in features. It seems no matter how a Chinese may live and dress so long as you know they Chinese. Then they are hated as one. There is not any right or justice for them.

May you Mr. Moulder [school superintendent], never be persecuted like the way you have persecuted little Mamie Tape.

Mamie Tape will never attend any of the Chinese schools of your making! Never!!! I will let the world see sir What justice there is When it is govern by the Race prejudice men!

Mrs. M. Tape

To subvert the legal judgment, the San Francisco board opened a segregated primary school for Chinese children. Despite Mrs. Tape's "Never!" she sent Mamie there, probably realizing that this legal battle might take decades and Mamie needed an education now.

PART FOUR

SETTLING THE WEST

They Wept Silently

When President Thomas Jefferson bought the western half of the Mississippi River Basin, known as the Louisiana Purchase, from France in 1803, he doubled the size of the United States. A year later Jefferson sent Meriwether Lewis and William Clark to explore the plains, cross over the Rockies to the Pacific Ocean, and make friendly contact with the Indians along the way. The explorers found a much-needed interpreter in Sacajawea, a Shoshoni Indian who had been captured in a clash between her people and another tribe, and later been sold or gambled away to a man named Toussaint Charbonneau, who was part Indian, part French Canadian. Charbonneau offered his wife's services as an interpreter even though she was pregnant at the time. Sacajawea gave birth along the way, rested for a few days, then strapped her baby to her back and continued on. During the two-and-a-half-year journey she washed laundry, gathered and cooked wild vegetables when food ran out, made moccasins when shoes gave out, and occasionally guided the men through unknown terrain. She proved invaluable when the expedition encountered Shoshoni Indians. Her brother was now a chief. He readily offered horses and helped the expedition navigate the Columbia and Clearwater Rivers.

Fur-trading companies quickly followed the trail west to the Pacific. Other Indian women found themselves willing and unwilling wives of trappers and traders. Very few white women would accompany men on such treacherous, primitive trips, and Indian women were more valuable companions anyway. They had already mastered the difficulties of wilderness living and could serve as negotiators and interpreters.

Catherine McDonald was the daughter of a Nez Perce woman and a man who was part Mohawk, part French or Scottish. In 1841 her fur-trapper father took her on an expedition in what is now the state of Idaho. Protected by her father, Catherine did not live in the double shadow of fear of being forcibly

taken as a wife or slave by a white man or being
attacked or murdered as other Indian women were.
Instead she was a witness to how the white man's
presence affected the lives of Indian women.

WE LEFT WHEN the antelope were fawning in the last month
of spring and the first of summer.

About 180 men sat and stood in groups chatting on the
prospects of the coming trip, as some chewed, others smoked,
and nearly all whittled in earnest anticipation of a voyage
whose ends they could not forsee. Although it promised
plenty of fur most of their wives refused to follow them
across. They were left to await our return.

[In a few days] we ascended a muddy little stream six
days from the Salt Lake. Scattered sage, juniper, nutwood
and willow were on our way. The natives were kind to us.
Their women were entirely nude save a short skirt of wolf
or rabbit skin which dropped from their hips to half their
length of thigh. They lived chiefly on wild fowl, roots, berries,
fish and bowskin and garter snakes. Their great enemies
were the Spaniards of Taos and California, who always
when they could, robbed them of their women and children,
leaving nothing but the men and the aged women, thus
making their desolation more disconsolate. Their captive
women were led to breed with their captors and to work
them and sell them like cattle. For these reasons they always
fled from us until they knew what we were, although some
of us were of similar brand.

Passing on for five further days, two Indian women were

found digging roots. They were seized and forced to join us. They wept silently and one of them pointed to her breasts, saying her child that sucked them would die if she left him, but our men took no heed of her. Next day her milk was streaming from her dugs and she became seriously sad, sobbing wildly and vehemently for her young, and I was bent on conniving at her escape. We also came upon three forsaken grass tents whose natives fled at our approach except two children, a boy and girl who had no mother, and their father being out hunting, the others left them to their fate. The poor motherless things were much frightened and nearly choked from fear, but a little rude tenderness and some food relieved them of their extreme emotion and in a few days their woeful alarm wore off and they came playful.

But the poor father, where was he and what a hopeless fire he must have lighted on the night of his return to his dark and grassy home.

We were now bearing southwest to west daily, the country becoming extremely barren of grass. We were two weeks without seeing an Indian, no fowl or any kind no hare nor reptile nor insect, a country that appeared to possess no life. [Then we met up with a party of Spaniards] driving a team of mules packed with Spanish blankets and on their way from Texas to California. The men looked poor and were afoot except the master, who was well horsed. They were driving a band of sheep for their food, killing daily in the evening.

With them we traveled two weeks and traded some beaver to them for blankets and a little flour. The women were horsed, but all the children that could walk walked barefooted and looked indigent and needy. Some girls there were going, as they said, to California to marry. The Spaniards had a guitar and a violin and the children, women and men sang and played every evening. They were happy. They had three Indian children they forced from their parents. In such actions causing the deepest woe on earth, they appeared to be callous and utterly feelingless. Our own party sold them the [Indian] children they stole.

The next day the trappers and the Spaniards separated. Four days later the trappers came upon a group of Indians who graciously received them. The visitors stayed and trapped more beavers. One morning four or five traps were missing.

THE TRAPPERS WERE enraged. My father's traps were never touched; he often found an Indian guarding his traps. He used to give the Indians all the beaver meat he and I did not consume. At last the trappers resolved to make a day of revenge for their five traps and designed to attack the Indians in their own camp unawares. My father was invited to join in the bloody work, but he refused saying, "I did not come here to war but to catch fur. These Indians may know nothing about your traps. They may have been taken by some distant thieves. Why arm to murder these poor hospitable people. They have no arms but clubs and bows."

Early the next morning before breakfast the party took to their arms. There was one low little cliff which overlooked the Indian camp and the river. Behind the top of it unseen the rifleman lay. The first shot fired was at an old grey-headed savage who was quietly taking his breakfast facing the sun in the door of his little home. He was struck in the ball of the knee and as he sat the ball followed and shattered to pieces his thigh bone. He fell backward and looked toward the cliff. The cry of alarm was out and high, and as the startled Indians stood to learn and look more the riflemen fired. Yells of woe from men, women and children filled the place. The dead and wounded lay there. The active ran to the river. Men, women and children plunged in and swam, but they were picked off by these cruel marksmen. The women made every effort to swim and save their children. Women who had one or two children made by terrible labor a safe landing with them on the other side, but those who had three and four children could not get over and gradually sank with them, going faithful to the death to what was their only solace and delight in that lonely valley.

The trappers after this work went into the deserted camp, pillaged everything they liked in it and killed the old Indian who was first hit in the knee. They then came back perfectly unconcerned and smoked and jested over the success of their revenge.

After this swift attack we left.

Left Our Hitherto Happy Home

The potential riches of furs, gold, and silver, along with governmental guarantees of free land, lured Americans west in the nineteenth century. The economic depression of 1837 dropped wages by as much as 50 percent and threw hundreds of thousands of Easterners out of work. They saw the west as a cure for personal and economic problems. Between 1840 and 1870, 350,000 people traveled by wagon to the California and Oregon territories. Thousands more stopped on the way and settled in Utah and Colorado. The completion of the transcontinental railroad in 1860 made it easier for later settlers to reach land in the Dakotas, Minnesota, Nebraska, Kansas, Montana, and southwestern Texas.

The migrants were usually families from small towns and rural areas in the midwest and upper south, but some came from as far as New York and Vermont. Unlike the early settlers in Virginia and New England, these settlers had to pay all their moving expenses. Depending on the starting point, the trip could cost from $500 to $1,500, the equivalent of two years' wages for a skilled craftsman. A suitable wagon had to be bought or built. Money was needed—for cattle, food, cooking equipment, rifles, gunpowder; for supplies along the way; and to tide the family over until the land turned a profit.

Missionary wives and nuns, bringing the word of God to Native Americans, eagerly journeyed west, but many married women did not share their husbands' enthusiasm to migrate. They did not want to leave their families, especially their mothers and sisters and other female relatives. They did not want to leave their women friends. On the frontier, who would share the joys and difficulties of pregnancy and childbirth and child rearing with them? Who would help them when there was sickness and trouble? Where would they find the comfort and fun of daily visits with their friends, who shared experiences that their husbands did not understand? The women resented being wrenched from their stable lives to the dangers and isolation of pioneer life. They feared disease and discomfort and Indian attacks along the way. Pregnant women feared miscarriages and the pain or danger of giving birth on the trail. And the frontier was not the proper place to bring up children. But their husbands wanted to go, and so they went.

The two-thousand mile Overland Trail officially began in towns along the Missouri River and followed the Platte River through Nebraska and Colorado to Wyoming, where the trail split. The south fork led to Salt Lake City, Utah, then through Nevada to Sacramento, California. The northern route led to Idaho and Oregon. Travelers started their six- to eight-month journey in April when the mud was hardening, hoping to arrive west before the trail was impassable due to snow and ice.

The trip was always grueling. Families rode ten hours a day in wagons with no springs, and under the wagon canvas temperatures could reach 110 degrees. Unexpected rains left everyone and everything damp. Dust storms parched throats and coated all possessions. Wagons had to be unloaded and reloaded when roads were unpassable. As a last resort, travelers abandoned their possessions, hoping to get to the next town alive.

Women performed their domestic chores on the move. They washed clothes on rocks in rivers, prepared meals in rain, baked bread over open fires, collected "buffalo chips" (dried manure) when wood could not be found. They entertained bored and irritable children. They nursed their families through fever, dysentery, and measles, and buried those who did not survive. They pitched tents, loaded and unloaded wagons, and drove ox teams. If their husbands died, they assumed total responsibility for the family.

In 1846 sixteen-year-old Mary Bailey and her husband, Dr. Frederick Bailey, moved from Vermont to Sylvania, Ohio. Five years later her husband decided to move to California. Despite Mary's ill health and lack of desire to do so, she dutifully packed up. The Baileys traveled along the Platte River to South Pass, then turned south to Salt Lake City and followed the California Road along the Humboldt River to Amador,

Gathering buffalo chips

California. This fragment from Mary Bailey's diary covers the first two and a half months of their journey west.

Wednesday, April 13, 1852

Left our hitherto happy home in Sylvania amid the tears and parting kisses of dear friends, many of whom were endeared to me by their kindness shown to me when I was a stranger in a strange land, when sickness and death visited our small family & removed our darling, our only child in a moment, as it were. Such kindness I can never forget. The sympathy I received from all was truly consoling & while life lasts will never be forgotten.

Monday, May 17, 1852

Went into the woods & slept out on the ground for the first time. It seemed as though it would kill us to sleep outdoors without anything but a canvas to protect us from the dews of Heaven, but it did not make any of us sick.

Tuesday, 18th.

Were up early to make a tent. It seemed hard to sit on the ground to sew. We would take a trunk or sack for a chair. Was very tired that night.

Friday, 21st.

Have traveled in the rain all day & we are stuck in the mud. I sit in the wagon writing while the men are at work doubling the teams to draw us out.

Tuesday, 25th.

Were nearly all day crossing [the Missouri]. Our men had to do all the work & we had to pay $10 besides. Camped on a high prairie without wood near for the first time.

Wednesday, 26th.

Saw *Wolves*. Fine roads & good weather. Some splendid scenery.

Friday, 28th.

I am lying under the wagon with my head on the saddle & the Dr's head on my lap. We have taken our lunch & are resting ourselves. The feed for the horses is as good as need be. All as need be except Sarah Withington who is very miserable. Her mother is suffering much on her account.

Sunday, 30th.

A day of rest. It does not seem much like keeping the Sabbath. The men are all airing their bed clothes. Many wash, bake & do all their work. I have not washed yet nor do I intend to on the Sabbath. We received a visit from an Indian early in the morning. He brought a paper stating that the tribe were in a very destitute condition. This one was nearly naked. At night 2 others came & slept under the wagons.

Tuesday, 1st of June.

We fought miskeetoos all night and early in the morning, we started to find a place to cook some breakfast & water our horses. We soon found a good place.

Wednesday, 3rd.*

Had a hard drive. Weather very warm. Saw a shower coming so we hurried to pitch our tent. We got our beds made in our tent when the lightening flashed & the thunder roared. I think I never witnessed a more terrific shower. It was as much as we could do to keep our tent from blowing over for some time. Were very glad to get a drink of tea & go to bed if not to sleep.

* From here on in the diary, Mary Bailey's dates conflict with the days of the week she assigned them.

Thursday, 4th.

It is cold enough to wear overcoats. 12:00 I am sitting on the banks of the Platte with my feet almost in the water. Have been writing to my Mother. How I wish some of my own relations could be with me.

Saturday, 5th.

This morning we came into the road that came from St. Joseph. Saw any quantity of teams, horses & oxen, mules, men, women & children. All pass through Fort Kearney. We left letter there. We went into the register office & looked over the names of those who had passed before us. Some 20,000 men, 6,000 women, besides cattle & horses, mules & sheep to almost any amount. We saw a great many new made graves. There had been a good deal of sickness on the St. Jo's road, almost every company had one or more.

Tuesday, 8th.

Eliza is quite sick & the Dr. has had a hard chill. I am sick, too. It seems rather hard. We did not drive more than 10 miles & stopped to get rested by a frog pond.

Wednesday, 9th.

Eliza is better today. What cause of gratitude we have that so many of us are well & are all spared while we pass so many new graves everyday. Still we have not seen a dead person.

Friday, 11th.

Very warm & dry, dusty. Nothing green to be seen excepting on the banks of the river. Fortunately for us, it is not very windy.

Do not feel well today. It is rather hard for me to ride

in a wagon & I feel the want of a chair when we stop. I like my sleeping room very well, that is the tent.

Saturday, 12th.

It was really amusing to see the men stand in the river to wash. They all acted so awkward.

Sunday, [June] 13th.

How thankful we ought to be for the Sabbath. None but an Infinite Being could have foreseen the absolute necessity of one day in seven for rest to man & beast. I never realized that good of a Sunday so much before.

Friday, 18th.

Very heavy sandy roads. Made up our mind to dispose of everything we can spare to make our freight less. I am writing to my dear parents for I well know how anxious they are on our account.

Saturday, 19th.

Left our trunks.

Monday, [July] 21st.

Crossed Scotts Bluffs & some of the most romantic scenery I ever *saw*. It would not require very great imagination, however, to think it some ancient city with high walls, great towers & every prerequisite to it.

The Baileys moved several times over the next eight years until they settled in Santa Cruz, California.

Four Walls and the Roof

In 1859, when Anna Howard Shaw was twelve years old, her father became a homesteader in northern

Michigan. Homesteading laws allowed a man to file a claim on a piece of land, paying a small sum per acre. The land became his if he cleared it, built a house on it, and farmed it for a certain number of years. The Federal Homestead Act of 1862 allowed single women over twenty-one, women who were heads of households, and women immigrants in the process of becoming citizens to acquire land too.

Anna Howard Shaw's father and her three oldest brothers cleared just enough land on their claim to put up the walls of a log cabin. James, the twenty-year-old son, stayed on; the others returned home to Lawrence, Massachusetts, to work in the textile mills. A few months later Mr. Shaw sent his wife and their

Pioneer family in front of their sod house

four youngest children to Michigan. Anna Howard
Shaw describes how shocked her mother was at what
she found and how it affected her. Life in Michigan
was as primitive as life had been in colonial America
200 years before.

WE ALL HAD an idea that we were going to a farm, and
we expected some resemblance at least to the prosperous
farms we had seen in New England. What we found awaiting
us were the four walls and the roof of a good-sized log-
house, standing in a small cleared strip of the wilderness,
its doors and windows represented by square holes, its floor
also a thing of the future, its whole effect achingly forlorn
and desolate. It was late in the afternoon when we drove
up to the opening that was its front entrance, and I shall
never forget the look my mother turned upon the place.
Without a word she crossed its threshold, and, standing
very still, looked slowly around her. Then something within
her seemed to give way, and she sank upon the ground.
She could not realize even then, I think, that this was really
the place father had prepared for us, that here he expected
us to live. When she finally took it in she buried her face
in her hands, and in that way she sat for hours without
moving or speaking. For the first time in her life she had
forgotten us; and we, for our part, dared not speak to
her. We stood around her in a frightened group, talking
to one another in whispers. Our little world had crumbled
under our feet. Never before had we seen our mother give
way to despair.

Night began to fall. The woods became alive with night creatures, and the most harmless made the most noise. The owls began to hoot, and soon we heard the wildcat, whose cry—a screech like that of a lost and panic-stricken child—is one of the most appalling sounds of the forest. Later the wolves added their howls to the uproar, but though darkness came and we children whimpered around her, our mother still sat in her strange lethargy.

[While my brother] was picketing the horses and building his protecting fires my mother came to herself, but her face when she raised it was worse than her silence had been. She seemed to have died and to have returned to us from the grave, and I am sure she felt that she had done so. From that moment she took up again the burden of her life, a burden she did not lay down until she passed away; but her face never lost the deep lines those first hours of her pioneer life had cut upon it.

[That night what] I most feared was within, not outside of, the cabin. The one sure refuge in our new world had been taken from us. I hardly knew the silent woman who lay near me, tossing from side to side and staring into the darkness; I felt that we had lost our mother.

[When my father] took up his claim, and sent [us] to live there alone until he could join us eighteen months later, he gave no thought of the manner in which we were to make the struggle and survive the hardships before us. He had furnished us with land and the four walls of a log cabin. We were one hundred miles from a railroad, forty miles from the nearest post-office, and half a dozen miles from any neighbors save Indians, wolves, and wildcats; we were wholly unlearned in the ways of the woods as well as in the most primitive methods of farming; we lacked not only every comfort, but even the bare necessities of life.

We faced our situation with clear and unalarmed eyes the morning after our arrival. We had brought with us enough coffee, pork, and flour to last for several weeks; and the one necessity father had put inside the cabin walls was a great fireplace, made of mud and stones, in which our food could be cooked. [We found] a creek a long distance from the house; and for months we carried from this creek, in pails, every drop of water we used, save that which we caught in troughs when the rain fell.

Obviously the first thing to do was to put doors and windows into the yawning holes father had left for them, and to lay a board flooring over the earth inside our cabin walls, and these duties we accomplished before we had occupied our new home a fortnight. [We made] three windows and two doors; then, inspired by these achievements, we ambitiously constructed an attic and divided the ground floor with partitions, which gave us four rooms.

The general effect was temperamental and sketchy. The boards which formed the floor were never even nailed down; they were fine, wide planks without a knot in them, and they looked so well that we merely fitted them together as closely as we could and lightheartedly let them go at that. Neither did we properly chink the house. Nothing is more comfortable than a log cabin which has been carefully built and finished; but for some reason—probably because there seemed always a more urgent duty calling to us around the corner—we never plastered our house at all. The result was that on many future winter mornings we awoke to find ourselves chastely blanketed by snow, while the only warm spot in our living-room was that directly in front of the fireplace, where great logs burned all day. Even there our faces scorched while our spines slowly congealed, until we learned to revolve before the fire like a bird upon a spit. No doubt we would have worked more thoroughly if my brother James, who was twenty years old and our tower of strength, had remained with us; but when we had been in our new home only a few months he fell ill and was forced to go East for an operation. He was never able to return to us, and thus my mother, we three young girls, and my youngest brother—Harry, who was only eight years old—made our fight alone until father came to us, more than a year later.

Mother was practically an invalid. She had a nervous affection which made it impossible for her to stand without the support of a chair. But she sewed with unusual skill, and it was due to her that our clothes, notwithstanding the strain to which we subjected them, were always in good condition. She sewed for hours every day, and she was able to move about the house, after a fashion, by pushing herself around on a stool which James made for her as soon as we arrived. He also built for her a more comfortable chair with a high back.

My brothers and I [did] the work out of doors. It was too late in the season for plowing or planting, even if we had possessed anything with which to plow, and, moreover, our so-called "cleared" land was thick with sturdy tree-stumps.

Harry and I gathered [gooseberries, raspberries, and

plums] on the banks of our creek. Harry also became an expert fisherman. We had no hooks or lines, but he took wires from our hoop-skirts and made snares at the ends of poles. My part was to stand on a log and frighten the fish out of their holes by making horrible sounds, which I did with impassioned earnestness. When the fish hurried to the surface of the water to investigate the appalling noises they had heard, they were easily snared by [Harry], who was very proud of his ability to contribute in this way to the family table.

During our first winter we lived largely on cornmeal, making a little journey of twenty miles to the nearest mill to buy it; but even at that we were better off than our neighbors, for I remember one family in our region who for an entire winter lived solely on coarse-grained yellow turnips, gratefully changing their diet to leeks when these came in the spring.

There Was a Prejudice Against Female Teachers

In 1830 author-educator Catharine Beecher left Hartford, Connecticut, and moved to Cincinnati, Ohio. Here she became convinced that there was a pressing need for women teachers for the children of the migrants moving west. Through the 1840s she traveled and lectured to win support for her idea. She insisted that teaching was the perfect profession for women, for it did not mean stepping out of their sphere. Teaching was a natural extension of women's roles as molders and nurturers of the young at home.

It was also a job that men seeking fortunes in the west did not want, for it was low-paying work. But for women interested in "doing good," or saving society, having respectable work was more important than high wages. When the Board of National Popular Education was founded in 1847, Beecher was put in charge of selecting, training, and placing teachers in western towns and cities.

Like Catharine Beecher, Ellen Lee believed that teaching was a Christian calling, her way of doing God's work. This belief sustained her when she was lonely and missed the comforts of home. It also gave her the strength to overcome the community's initial prejudice against the new teacher, who was a woman instead of a man.

Hamilton County, Indiana
January 6, 1852

Dear Friends,

I have just commenced the second term of my school here, so that I am able to judge pretty correctly of my prospects in this place.

It is a new settlement here, it being only fifteen years since the first person settled here. But the settlement is quite large, and thickly settled.

Nearly all live in log-houses. The people are kind to me, very kind; they are peaceful, honest, intelligent naturally, but have not had an opportunity for improving their minds; so that they are very ignorant. I have not seen a well-educated person; many of the adults can neither read nor write, and some cannot tell one letter from another, and do not care if the children cannot. There are nine preachers here, and scarcely one can read a chapter in the Bible correctly; and I have heard most of them preach; they are not at all like New England ministers and it is often a cross to hear them preach: but I hope some of them are good Christian men, who try to perform their duty, and not only preach, but practice what they preach.

Just before I came here, a Sabbath School had been organized, and they had purchased a library of some more than 100 volumes; when I came here they were on the point of giving it up. They consented to try it longer.

We have now divided it into classes. I am obliged to take charge of all the females, there being no one else who can; and sometimes I have a great number, and of course can not do as I would; and beside they depend on me to assist the others, but I enjoy it much; in this way some can be taught, who can be taught in no other way. It now seems prosperous and the interest increasing; sometimes the house is nearly full of children. Some of the parents who at first felt no interest in it, say they would rather give up anything than the Sabbath School. I hope the interest will continue to increase, and that it will prove a blessing to the neighborhood.

I came here unexpected by the people, but I was received

kindly. My school was not very large at first, but it has gradually increased, 'till I have now about 50 pupils most of whom are between the ages of 14 and 22. There has been no school here before for more than a year, and they have never had a teacher who could do more than read, write and cipher a little; and these he did very imperfectly, so that my scholars are very backward but they are eager to learn, bright, active, attentive, and obedient, and learn very fast. I have a large number of young men between the ages of 18 and 21; they are very respectful, and obedient.

I think I have gained the respect and affection of all my pupils, so that their obedience is cheerfully given. When I came here, there was a prejudice against female teachers; they had always employed men, and had never had a school six weeks without trouble, and they thought of course, if a man could not govern their boys, a woman could not; but I was allowed to take my own course, and I gave them only one rule, that was—Do right. And by awakening their consciences to a sense of right and wrong, and other similar influences, I have succeeded much better than I expected, and have had to use no other influences than kindness. The parents have been interested to visit the school, and I find this the best way, and the surest way to interest them.

In my school I am content, and happy for I hope I am doing good, but I am entirely deprived of sympathy, and good society. I have no human being here, in whom I can confide, or who possesses kindred feelings with mine. Were it not that I can cast all my care on God, and go to his Word for sympathy and consolation, I should be unhappy.

I am also deprived of many New England comforts, and

nearly all its privileges, but when I think that I am giving a privilege to others, which they have never enjoyed I think I ought not to complain. But although I sometimes sigh, and long for christian sympathy, and the privileges I once enjoyed, and feel lonely when I think of home, and friends, yet I am happy. If I can in my way be useful I shall be happy. Pray for me, that my coming here may not be in vain. I should be pleased to hear from you.

Yours truly, Ellen P. Lee

By the time of Civil War, one out of four teachers was a woman; yet female teachers earned half what male teachers earned. By 1870 two out of three elementary school teachers were women; their wages were still less than male teachers'.

Hogs in My Kitchen

In 1848 gold was discovered in California. The idea that riches could be gotten with only a pick and shovel and a pan was infectious and irresistible. Within a year the population of the California territory jumped from 40,000 to 100,000. And in four years it had doubled. Prospectors came from the east and from Europe seeking gold, but few found the riches they had fantasized about. Some women saw the Gold Rush as an opportunity to make money serving the prospectors. They went west to set up boardinghouses and hotels. These lodgings were often no more than canvas tents on poles, but feeding three meals a day to thirty miners could bring in $30 a day, or $480 a month, a great deal of money in those days. Women added to their earnings by washing, ironing, sewing, and caring for children.

On December 9, 1851, Mary Ballou and her husband left their two children behind in Alexandria, New Hampshire, to begin their two-month trip to California. On December 11 they sailed from New York City to the Isthmus of Panama, which they crossed with mules and on foot. They continued by ship up the coast of California. On January 11 they arrived in a California mining camp. In a letter to her son written nine months later, Ballou vividly describes her life out west. Her loneliness and worries about her children suggest that only economic necessity separated her from them.

California Negrobar
October 30, 1852

My Dear Selden

we are about as usual in health. well I suppose you would like to know what I am doing in this gold region. well I will try to tell you what my work is here in this muddy Place. All the kitchen that I have is four posts stuck down

into the ground and covered over the top with factory cloth
no floor but the ground. this is a Boarding House kitchen.
there is a floor in the dining room and my sleeping room
covered with nothing but cloth.

Oct 27 this morning I awoke and it rained in torrents.
well i got up and I thought of my House. I went and
looket into my kitchen. the mud and water was over my
Shoes I could not go into the kitchen to do any work to
day but kept perfectly dry in the Dining so I got along
very well. your Father put on his Boots and done the work
in the kitchen. I felt badly to think that I was de[s]tined
to be in such a place. I wept for a while and then I commenced
singing and made up a song as I went along.

now I will try to tell you what my work is in this Boarding
House. well somtimes I am washing and Ironing somtimes
I am making mince pie and Apple pie and squash pies.
Somtimes frying mince turnovers and Donuts. I make Buis-
cuit and now and then Indian jonny cake and then again I
am making minute puding filled with rasons and Indian
Bake pudings and then again a nice plum Puding and then
again I am Stuffing a Ham of pork that cost forty cents a
pound. three times a day I set my Table which is about
thirty feet in length and do all the little fixings about it
such as filling pepper boxes and vinegar cruits and mustard
pots and Butter cups. somtimes I am feeding my chickens
and then again I am scareing the Hogs out of my kitchen
and Driving the mules out of my Dining room.

you can see by the descrption of that I have given you
of my kitchen that anything can walk into the kitchen that
choeses to walk in and there being no door to shut from

the kitchen into the Dining room you see that anything can walk into the kitchen and then from kitchen into the Dining room so you see the Hogs and mules can walk in any time day or night if they choose to do so. somtimes I am up all times a night scaring the Hogs and mules out of the House. last night there a large rat came down pounce down onto our bed in the night.

sometimes I take my fan and try to fan myself but I work so hard that my Arms pain me so severely that I kneed some one to fan me so I do not find much comfort anywhere. somtimes I am taking care of Babies and nursing at the rate of Fifty Dollars a week but I would not advise any Lady to come out here and suffer the toil and fatigue that I have suffered for the sake of a little gold.

Clarks Simmon wife says if she was safe in the States she would not care if she had not one cent. She came in here last night and said, "Oh dear I am so homesick that I must die," and then again my other associate came in with tears in her eyes and said that she had cried all day. she said if she had as good a home as I had got she would not stay twenty five minutes in California. I told her that she could not pick up her duds in that time. she said she would not stop for duds nor anything else but my own heart was two sad to cheer them much.

October 21 well I have been to church to hear a methodist sermon. his Text was let us lay aside every weight and the sin that doth so easely beset us. I was the only Lady that was present and about forty gentleman. So you see that I go to church when I can.

I will tell you a little of my bad feelings. on the 9 of

September there was a little fight took place in the store.
I saw them strike each other through the window in the
store. one went and got a pistol and started towards the
other man. I never go into the store but your mothers
tender heart could not stand that so I ran into the store
and Beged and plead with him not to kill him for eight or
ten minutes not to take his Life for the sake of his wife
and three little children to spare his life and then I ran
through the Dining room into my sleeping room and Buried
my Face in my bed so as not to hear the sound of the
pistol and wept Biterly. Oh I thought if I had wings how
quick I would fly to the States. that night at the supper
table he told the Boarders if it had not been for what that
Lady said to him Scheles would have been a dead man.

there I hear the Hogs in my kichen turning the Pots
and kettles upside down so I must drop my pen and drive
them out. so you this is the way I have to write—jump up
every five minutes for somthing and then again I washed
out about a Dollars worth of gold dust the fourth of July
in the cradles so you see that I am doing a little mining in
this gold region but I think it harder to rock the cradle to
wash out gold than it is to rock the cradle for the Babies
in the States.

I have no windows in my room. all the light that I have
shines through canvas that covers the House and my eyes
are so dim that I can hardly see to make a mark so I
think you will excuse me for not writing any better. I have
three Lights burning now but I am so tired and Blind that
I can scearcely see and here I am among the French and
Duch and Scoth and Jews and Italions and Sweeds and

Chineese and Indians and all manner of tongus and nations but I am treated with due respect by all of them.

I immagine you will say what a long yarn this is from California. if you can read it all I must close soon for I am so tired and almost sick. Oh my Dear Selden I am so Home sick I will say to you once more to see that Augustus has everything that he kneeds to make him comfortable and by all means have him Dressed warm this cold winter. I worry a great deal about my Dear children. it seems as though my heart would break when I realise how far I am from my Dear Loved ones this from your affectionate mother

Mary B Ballou

In America There Was a Great Deal of Gold

In 1850 California had about 12 men to every woman. Single and young, usually fifteen to twenty-four years old, the prospectors were delighted with women like Mary Ballou who performed domestic chores for them and equally delighted by the women who served their sexual needs. Prostitutes came from the United States and as far away as Germany, Spain, Chile, France, and China. Unlike the European and American prostitutes, who often chose to go west, most Chinese women came against their will. By 1854 Chinese prostitution in San Francisco was big business, controlled by Chinese men. Chinese brothel owners

sent agents to China to find young girls. In the nineteenth century Chinese peasants often found themselves
without enough money to feed their families, even
after a year of hard work. Since men carried on the
ancestral line, during these difficult economic times
girls of poor families, more than boys, were sacrificed
to help the family survive. Parents often sold their
six-year-old daughters as domestic servants. These
girls were resold as prostitutes when they were older.

But agents often failed to get enough young girls.
When persuasion failed, agents deceived or kidnapped
young girls, just as they had done during colonial
times when the pool of indentured servants shrank.
Forced into prostitution, these young girls saw none
of the profits they generated.

An unknowing victim, Wong Ah So, explains how
she ended up in the United States in the late nineteenth
century.

I WAS BORN in Canton Province, my father was sometimes
a sailor and sometimes he worked on the docks, for we
were very poor.

I was nineteen when this man came to my mother and
said that in America there was a great deal of gold. Even
if I just peeled potatoes there, he told my mother I would

earn seven or eight dollars a day, and if I was willing to do any work at all I would earn lots of money. He was a laundryman, but said he earned plenty of money. He was very nice to me, and my mother liked him, so my mother was glad to have me go with him as his wife.

I thought I was his wife, and was very grateful that he was taking me to such a grand, free country, where everyone was rich and happy.

When we first landed in San Francisco we lived in a hotel in Chinatown, a nice place, but one day, after I had been there for about two weeks, a woman came to see me. She was young, very pretty, and all dressed in silk. She told me that I was not really Huey Yow's wife, but she had asked him to buy her a slave, that I belonged to her, and must go with her, but she would treat me well, and I could buy back my freedom, if I was willing to please, and be agreeable, and she would let me off in two years, instead of four if I did not make a fuss. She said that so I would be quieter about it. I did not believe her, I thought she was lying to me. So when Huey Yow came I asked him why that woman had come and what she meant by all that lying. But he said that it was true; that he was not my husband, he did not care about me, and that this was something that happened all the time. Everybody did this, he said, and why be so shocked that I was to be a prostitute instead of a married woman. I asked him, "What is a prostitute? Am I not your wife?" And he said, "Couldn't I just say that you were my wife? That does not make it so. Everybody does this sort of thing. The woman gave me money to bring you over."

Ah So was forced to become a prostitute. At a party seven months later she met a friend of her father's. He questioned her about her present life and she explained how she and the family had been deceived. Within two weeks Ah So was rescued by Chinese and American members of a San Francisco mission headed by Donaldina Cameron. From 1875 to 1938, reformer Cameron crusaded to free Chinese girls and prostitutes from virtual slavery.

A Time Never to Be Forgotten

While Mary Ballou lived among the hogs in her kitchen in California, Maria Ascension Sepulveda y Avila led a comfortable life as the daughter of a wealthy cattle rancher. Ascension's grandparents were among the first Spanish settlers in the pueblo of Los Angeles in the 1780s and gradually acquired substantial land holdings. In 1837 Ascension's father added 48,000 acres to his grazing lands. Within ten years, with the influx of prospectors and settlers, he found a ready, lucrative market for his cattle, and made his fortune.

Ascension, the twelfth of thirteen children, was born in 1844. She spent most of her childhood with her oldest sister and her sister's husband, who lived in the family townhouse in Los Angeles. From age nine to sixteen she was sent to a convent school. When she was almost sixteen, she met her future husband, thirty-year-old Thomas Mott. Ascension describes her courtship and marriage to Mott in the well-chaperoned world of Spanish tradition.

THE FIRST TIME I saw the man who was later to become my husband was when I was seven years old. My father had imported a fine race horse from Australia, the "Black Swan." The groom was accustomed to lead him around the corral for exercises, and frequently I was allowed to sit upon his back.

The gentlemen of the neighborhood used to come and watch the "Black Swan." One day came Mr. Thomas Mott. Even at that first sight of him I was impressed by his distinguished appearance.

He had come to San Francisco from New York in the year 1849 with the rush of gold seekers, making the journey by way of the Isthmus of Panama. In the year 1852 he came to Los Angeles and established himself in business.

The [third] time I saw Mr. Mott was just after I left the Convent in San Jose. I was barely sixteen and had been taken to my first ball by my sister. The only reason my sister took me was because there was no one at home with whom I could stay.

There were many guests, and I sat between my sister and my cousin. Dr. Winston, an old friend of the family, was standing near us and with him was a very handsome gentleman. They had been glancing in our direction for some time, so my cousin said, when finally they walked over and spoke to my sister and my cousin, apparently not noticing me at all. They exchanged a few remarks and then suddenly and to my extreme [embarrassment], Dr. Winston's friend, who was none other than Mr. Mott, leaned over and broke several handfuls of "cacarones" (confetti) on my head. The confetti was made from gilt paper and I was covered with the shimmering bits from the braids wound around my head to the hem of my ruffled white silk dress. Without a word Mr. Mott bowed and walked away. I was fresh from the Convent and I thought that the gentleman had very strange manners indeed.

Shortly after this incident Mr. Mott called upon my mother and father and told them that he would like to marry me and asked their permission to court me. My parents replied that I was very young but that he might call on me.

During his ensuing visits I never saw him alone. The room was always filled with members of my family and his remarks were chiefly addressed to them. My brother, Joaquin, was the only one of my brothers and sisters to favor Mr. Mott's suit. The others put as many obstacles in his way as possible.

I attended a ball at the Prudhomme home on one occasion and they surrounded me with people and arranged to have my dance program filled as quickly as possible so that Mr. Mott would be unable to obtain a dance with me. However, his good friend, Dr. Winston, gave him his dance with me, and presently Mr. Mott walked over to me and asked if I would grant him the favor of a dance. I replied that I was sorry but I was afraid I had none left and then he explained Dr. Winston's kindness.

Whenever Mr. Mott called to take me riding I was always accompanied by some of my women relations, one of whom sat in the front seat with him. On one occasion, just as my sister, Francisca, was about to occupy the front seat as usual, my kind cousin Josefa pulled her back and insisted on my being permitted to sit with Mr. Mott. I was forbidden however to speak any English as they could not understand it, and as Mr. Mott spoke little Spanish it can be readily imagined that the conversation lagged somewhat. However, he managed to write a little poem on a scrap of paper and hand it to me surreptitiously. I tucked it away in my dress and later read it in the privacy of my boudoir. I still have the paper to this day.

Shortly after this Mr. Mott asked if he might see me alone to ask for my hand in marriage. It was willingly granted as they thought from my assumed indifference that I would refuse him. I did refuse him this time telling him that I was too young and that I was not going to think of marriage for a while. I was very touched by his unhappiness when he left me and gave him a flower from the garden.

He went to Santa Barbara soon after and those who were opposed to the match saw to it that rumors reached my ears that [he] was paying a great deal of attention to certain other young ladies, which of course did not add to my happiness.

Pio Pico was a good friend of ours, and Mr. Mott finally enlisted his aid. It happened that the Carlisles' first son was to be christened and Mr. Pico arranged that Mr. Mott should call to ask me to be godmother. There were many guests at the ceremony and when Mr. Mott and I arrived the Priest, Father Blas Rho, called out to us before them all and asked if we wished him to marry us.

Soon after this Mr. Mott presented an engagement ring to my father and mother and they placed it upon my finger. Mr. Mott then left for San Francisco. I did not even kiss him good-bye as I did not consider it proper until after I should become his wife.

In the meantime, women from Sonora came down to the ranch to sew my trousseau. My lingerie was made of linen and trimmed with drawn-work. My dresses and the rest of my things came from San Francisco.

Mr. Mott came down from San Francisco in time to attend a ball given in our honor on the 8th of December at the Bella Union. I had been down on the ranch overseeing the making of my trousseau, and rode the whole distance of thirty-five miles back to town on horseback in the pouring rain. When I arrived home, I was too utterly exhausted to attend the ball, which proceeded to be given without its guest of honor.

I was married at eight o'clock in the evening on December 23, 1861, at the home of my parents. My father had sent to Santa Barbara for the musicians, eight in number. The wonderful cakes and other things for the supper which followed the ceremony were all brought from San Francisco. Lanterns were strung all about the grounds giving a very gay effect.

My wedding gown was of white silk made with three flounces which were bordered with blocks of satin. The veil was of Alençon lace, and my wreath and bouquet were of artificial flowers.

My attendants were my cousin and Mrs. Carlisle. [One

wore a gown] of white silk made with three flounces of lace embroidered in colors; [the other's] gown was of wine colored velvet.

We were married by Father Blas Rho.

Immediately after the super we all went over to the Bella Union Hotel for the ball which was given us by Mr. Mott's friends. It was a very gay occasion. The guests were many and from all parts of California. At one time eighty couples were dancing the contra-dance.

My husband and I remained at the Hotel after the ball. The wedding guests from out of town were obliged to remain for six weeks as it rained without stopping the better part of that time, and the country was so flooded that it was impossible to reach San Pedro whence the steamer sailed once a month. My father's house was overflowing with guests and as the musicians were among those detained by the floods, the better part of the time was spent in dancing and gaiety. It was a time never to be forgotten.

PART FIVE

WORK AND POLITICS

An Unfortunate Victim

Throughout the nineteenth century, as America continued its rapid industrialization, workers' unions grew to help workers collectively resist unbearable working conditions.

The Working Women's Union, formed in 1864 by sewing and machine operators in New York City, spawned similar groups in Boston, Philadelphia, and Chicago. A committee of Philadelphia women visited President Lincoln and told him of their low wages and poor working conditions working for private employers under contract for the federal government. The President directed the official in charge of government contracts to remedy the situation.

Women shoe workers in Lynn, Massachusetts; collar laundresses in Troy, New York; factory workers in Dover, New Hampshire; women weavers in Fall River, Massachusetts; and washerwomen in Jackson, Mississippi, formed their own unions. The Working Women's Protective Union was organized and led by middle- and upper-middle-class women in the 1880s. It provided free legal services to help women workers recover unpaid wages, lobbied for laws to penalize employers who did not pay their workers, and found jobs for women.

The Knights of Labor, organized in 1869, was the first large-scale labor federation in the United States. From its beginning it stated the need for women and men to receive equal pay for equal work, but not until 1881 were women actively encouraged to join its local assemblies. By 1886 there were over 113 women's assemblies. That same year Leonora Barry, a hosiery worker from New York, was asked by the federation to head a department of women's work. For three years Barry traveled around the country, speaking to women factory workers, many of whom had sent letters asking for help in organizing assemblies. Where she wasn't invited, she tried to get into factories to investigate working conditions. She was often refused entrance. Women workers often hesitated to talk with her for fear of being fired. In a report, Barry describes wages and working conditions in a factory in Auburn, New York, in 1887.

WENT TO AUBURN, N.Y., Feb. 20, I found the working-women of this city in a deplorable state, there being none of them organized. There were long hours, poor wages and the usual results consequent upon such a condition. Not among male employers alone in this city, but a woman in whose heart we would expect to find a little pity and compassion for the suffering of her own sex. To the contrary, on this occasion, however, I found one who, for cruelty and harshness toward employees, has not an equal on the pages of labor's history—one who owns and conducts an establishment in which is manufactured women's and children's wear. Upon accepting a position in her factory an employee is compelled to purchase a sewing machine from the proprietress, who is agent for the S.M. Co. This must be paid for in weekly payments of 50 cents, provided the operative makes $3. Should she make $4 the weekly payment is 75 cents. At any time before the machine is paid for, through a reduction of the already meager wages, or the enforcement of some petty tyrannical rule—sickness, anger or any cause, the operative leaves her employ, she forfeits the machine and all the money paid upon it, and to the next applicant the machine is resold. She must purchase the thread for doing the work, as she is an agent for a thread company. It takes four spools of thread at 50 cents a spool to do $5 worth of work, and when $2 is paid for thread, and 50 cents for the machine, the unfortunate victim has $2.50 therewith to board, clothe and care for herself generally; and it is only experts who can make even this. Many other equally unjust systems are resorted to of which lack of space forbids mention.

I succeeded in organizing two Local Assemblies in this city, one of wood-workers, and one women's Local Assembly, numbering at organization 107 members, which has grown rapidly and is now one of the most flourishing Local Assemblies in the State.

And Learn of Life from Life Itself

By the end of the nineteenth century, despite the proliferation of women's colleges and the pathbreaking work of such women as Dr. Elizabeth Blackwell, ministers Olympia Brown and Anna Howard Shaw, and lawyers Lavinia Goodell and Belva Lockwood, inroads into the professions remained negligible for women. After completing college most educated women found themselves without careers.

In 1881, Jane Addams graduated from Rockford Seminary in Illinois. She had been an accomplished student and an admired student leader. She enrolled in medical school, but dropped out after a month due to illness. For the next four years Addams fell into a pattern familiar to single, educated women with no work. She took a grand tour of Europe with her stepmother and friends. She entertained guests at home, attended lectures, and did charity work. But the absence of a purpose in life shamed and depressed her.

On a second trip to Europe in 1887–88, Addams visited Toynbee Hall in London's poor East End and was greatly impressed by the work of this pioneering settlement house. A year later Addams and her friend Ellen Starr rented a house in Chicago's 19th Ward and created a new profession in the United States, the settlement worker. Settlement workers set out to solve urban problems brought about by industrialization. Their work was part of a larger reform movement that continued until the 1920s. In 1891 Addams' Hull House was the only settlement house in the United States. By 1910 there were 400 others.

Hull House became a haven for the immigrants who lived and worked in its surrounding tenements and shanties. Hull House workers helped them get medical care, education, emergency food, and employment, at a time when no government agencies existed to help them. Immigrant children attended the Hull House kindergarten and after-school clubs. Adults took classes in nutrition and household management, enjoyed literary evenings and concerts, and attended union meetings.

Jane Addams

Hull House was also a haven for its settlement workers, mostly educated single women from wealthy families. Living and working at Hull House provided them with meaningful work and a sense of community. They received no salaries for their work and paid room and board to live on the premises. The persistence and dedication of these women in helping those who were less fortunate often led to much-needed changes in government policy. Hull House became a model and inspiration for settlement work around the world. Many Hull House "graduates" became leaders in city, state, and federal government.

In her autobiography Addams describes her feelings during the eight years before she opened Hull House.

IT [TOOK] EIGHT years—from the time I left Rockford in the autumn of 1881 until Hull-House was opened in the autumn of 1889—to formulate my convictions even in the least satisfactory manner, much less to reduce them to a plan for action. During most of that time I was absolutely at sea so far as any moral purpose was concerned, clinging only to the desire to live in a really living world and refusing to be content with a shadowy intellectual or æsthetic reflection of it.

For two years there was mingled a sense of futility, of misdirected energy, the belief that the pursuit of cultivation would not in the end bring either solace or relief. I gradually reached a conviction that the first generation of college women had taken their learning too quickly, had departed too suddenly from the active emotional life led by their grandmothers and great-grandmothers; that the contemporary education of young women had developed too exclusively the power of acquiring knowledge and of merely receiving impression; that somewhere in the process of "being educated" they had lost that simply and almost automatic response to the human appeal, that old healthful reaction resulting in activity from the mere presence of suffering or of helplessness; that they are so sheltered and pampered they have no chance even to make "the great refusal."

It is hard to tell just when the very simple plan which afterward developed into the Settlement began to form itself in my mind. I gradually became convinced that it would be a good thing to rent a house in a part of the city where many primitive and actual needs are found, in which young women who have been given over too exclusively to study might restore a balance of activity along traditional lines and learn of life from life itself; where they might try out some of the things they had been taught and put truth to "the ultimate test of the conduct it dictates or inspires."

I had made up my mind that whatever happened, I would begin to carry out the plan, if only by talking about it. I can well recall the stumbling and uncertainty with which I finally set it forth to Miss Starr, my old-time school friend. I even dared to hope that she might join in carrying out the plan, but nevertheless I told it in the fear of that disheartening experience which is so apt to afflict our most cherished plans when they are at last divulged, when we suddenly feel that there is nothing there to talk about, and as the golden dream slips through our fingers we are left to wonder at our own fatuous belief. But gradually the comfort of Miss Starr's companionship, the vigor and enthusiasm which she brought to bear upon it, told both in the growth of the plan and upon the sense of its validity.

So it finally came about that in June, 1888, I found myself equipped with high expectations and a certain belief that whatever perplexities and discouragement concerning the life of the poor were in store for me, I should at least know something at first hand and have the solace of daily activity. I had confidence that although life itself might contain many difficulties, the period of mere passive receptivity had come to an end, and I had last finished with the everlasting "preparation for life," however ill-prepared I might be.

Nothing to Look Forward to

In 1860 women constituted only 10 percent of the work force, but by 1900 five million women, 20 percent of America's wage earners, worked for pay. Thirty-three percent of these women were domestic servants and waitresses; 25 percent were factory and mill workers; 10 percent, saleswomen and clerks; 10 percent, farmers; and 10 percent were professionals, mostly teachers. The remaining 12 percent worked at home, laundering and sewing and taking care of boarders.

Starting in the 1880s and continuing until World War I, millions of immigrants came to American cities in the northeast and midwest. They came in waves, from southern and eastern Europe and from Russia. Blacks from the rural south also went north seeking a better life. Married immigrant women tended to work at home, rolling cigars, making artificial flowers, and doing piecework sewing. Their daughters and other single women worked in factories. They braided and twisted cables, made matches, wove textiles, cleaned and packed fish, washed bottles, cut and labeled tin cases, packed meat and crackers, sorted feathers, stripped tobacco leaves, and trimmed and finished garments. Sexual discrimination excluded them from the higher-paying jobs in heavy industries such as shipbuilding, construction, and electrical work. Ethnic prejudice excluded immigrant women from being hired as clerks, typists, telegraph operators, and saleswomen. Racism excluded black women from factories and forced them into domestic service.

Factory work meant long hours, dangerous conditions, low wages, and unsanitary workplaces. Dust filled the air in feather, fur, and cotton factories. Women fainted in the heat and dampness of ill-ventilated laundries. Poorly designed and maintained machines injured hands, fingers, and arms. And, worst of all, workers had no legal protection from these hazards of the workplace.

The women stayed in these hazardous jobs despite the low pay because they had no other choices. Their families needed their paltry salaries to survive. Young women saw their work as temporary, until the family was established in the new country and until they got married.

By 1909 35,000 women, mostly Jewish and Italian immigrants, worked in shirtwaist factories in New York City. The shirtwaist was the most popular outfit of saleswomen, stenographers, office clerks, and teachers. This white blouse was pleated in front with a row of tucks and buttoned in the back. Women wore it with a long dark skirt or bought a shirtwaist dress with the skirt attached. Pauline Newman, a shirtwaist worker

Making cigars, Pittsburgh, Pennsylvania, 1909

and organizer for the International Ladies Garment Workers Union, describes life in the Triangle Shirtwaist Company factory.

THE TRIANGLE SHIRTWAIST Company was a family affair, all relatives of the owners running the place, watching to see that you did your work, watching when you went into the toilet. And if you were two or three minutes longer than foremen or foreladies thought you should be, it was deducted from your pay. If you came five minutes late in the morning because the freight elevator didn't come down to take you up in time, you were sent home for a half a day without pay.

Rubber heels came into use around that time and our employers were the first to use them; you never knew when they would sneak up on you, spying, to be sure you did not talk to each other during working hours.

Most of the women rarely took more than $6.00 a week home, most less. The early sweatshops were usually so dark that gas jets burned day and night. There was no insulation in the winter, only a pot-bellied stove in the middle of the factory. If you were a finisher and could take your work with you, you could sit next to the stove in winter. But if you were an operator or trimmer it was very cold indeed. Of course in the summer you suffocated with practically no ventilation.

There was no drinking water, maybe a tap in the hall, warm, dirty.

The condition was no better and no worse than the tenements where we lived. I lived in a two-room tenement with my mother and two sisters and the bedroom had no windows, the facilities were down in the yard, but that's the way it was in the factories too.

There was nothing to look forward to, nothing to expect the next day to be better.

Someone once asked me: "How did you survive?" And I told him, what alternative did we have? You stayed and you survived, that's all.

This Is Not the First Time

Settlement workers, reformers, and journalists alerted the public to the inhumanity of factory work and pressured the government to investigate working conditions and pass protective legislation. But too often the new laws were inadequately enforced. In 1903 a group of middle-class women formed the National Women's Trade Union League of America (NWTUL) to organize working women into unions, to lobby for protective laws, and to educate working women to run their own unions. Its first president was Mary Kehew, a wealthy Bostonian who was experienced in organizing women workers. The first vice president was Jane Addams. Union leaders such as Pauline Newman, Agnes Nestor, president of the International Glove Workers Union, and Rose Schneiderman, organizer of the Cap Workers Union, joined the NWTUL. The New York branch of the NWTUL was particularly effective in helping immigrant shirtwaist workers to organize a severely needed union in New York City.

In July 1909 disgust with low wages led two hundred employees of the Rosen Brothers Shirtwaist Company to strike. They won a 20-percent wage increase and the right for their union to bargain collectively for them. Their success spurred other workers to organize and strike. Owners hired guards to intimidate strikers and break picket lines so strikebreakers could enter the factories. Police harassed women picketeers with arrests on false charges. Despite the harassment, more workers joined the union.

On November 23, 3,000 workers met at Cooper Union Hall in New York City to discuss calling a general strike. Samuel Gompers, president of the American Federation of Labor, cautioned against it. Clara Lemlich, a fifteen-year-old striker recovering from a beating she had received on the picket line, roused the workers when she spoke: "I am tired of listening to speakers who talk in general terms. What we are here for is to decide whether we shall or shall not strike. I offer a resolution that a general strike be declared—now." The resolution was unanimously carried.

The next morning 20,000 workers left their jobs. The union had expected no more than a few thousand would strike. Within a week 30,000 were out on strike. Production stopped in 640 factories. Some small businesses gave in quickly, but the larger ones held out. Despite harassment, beatings, arrests, and starvation, the women stuck together. Members of the NWTUL picketed with the strikers and raised money so workers and their families would not starve.

On February 15, 1910, the shirtwaist strike was officially called off, even though 1,000 workers were still on strike. Most of the workers' demands had been met by the factory owners. The Triangle company, however, was one of the thirteen companies that had hired enough strikebreakers to defeat the workers, so when Triangle workers returned to work, they had no union agreement. While other workers had won a fifty-four-hour week, Triangle workers still worked fifty-nine hours. A key demand that factory workers be able to unlock exit doors usually kept locked from the outside, and that fire escapes be workable, had never been discussed.

On March 25, 1911, a fire broke out on the eighth floor of the building that housed the Triangle company. Workers tried to open the locked doors to get to the outside and use the fire escapes but most couldn't. Fire escapes broke under their weight. Out of 500 workers, 146 died: 143 women and girls, and three men, jumped to their deaths or were burned or suffocated. Their charred and bloody bodies covered the sidewalks.

These deaths moved even people who had been unsympathetic to the strike. A memorial meeting, sponsored by the NWTUL, was held at the Metropolitan Opera House. At the meeting, resolutions demanding a fire-prevention bureau, additional fire inspectors, and new legislation were booed down by angry workers. Rose Schneiderman spoke from the podium. She echoed the feelings of the crowd that too little had been offered too late:

I WOULD BE a traitor to these poor burned bodies if I came here to talk good fellowship. We have tried you good people of the public and we have found you wanting. This is not the first time girls have been burned alive in the city. Every week I must learn of the untimely death of one of my sister workers. Every year thousands of us are maimed. The life of men and women is so cheap and property is so sacred. There are so many of us for one job it matters little if 143 [women] are burned to death.

We have tried you, citizens; we are trying you now, and you have a couple of dollars for the sorrowing mothers and daughters and sisters by way of a charity gift. But every time the workers come out in the only way they know to protest against conditions which are unbearable, the strong hand of the law is allowed to press down heavily upon us.

Public officials have only words of warning to us—warning that we must be intensely orderly and must be intensely peaceable, and they have the workhouse just back of all their warnings. The strong hand of the law beats us back when we rise into the conditions that make life bearable.

I can't talk fellowship to you who are gathered here. Too much blood has been spilled. I know from my experience it is up to the working people to save themselves. The only way they can save themselves is by a strong working-class movement.

Is Peace More a Concern of Women?

By the end of the nineteenth century hundreds of thousands of white middle-class women belonged to women's associations and clubs whose concerns ranged from temperance to suffrage, to settlement houses, to college educations for women, to world peace. Black women's clubs were also involved in antilynching activities and providing leadership for other black women.

In 1915, unsatisfied with pacifist organizations already in existence and dominated by men, a group of prominent women—including Jane Addams, Carrie Chapman Catt, President of the National Woman Suffrage Association, and lawyer-reformer Crystal Eastman—helped organize the Woman's Peace Party (WPP). The women saw themselves as "custodians of life" who "revolted against both the cruelty and waste of war" and could "no longer consent to its reckless destruction." The Women's Peace Party continued speaking out against war even after the United States became involved in World War I. This angered some Americans, who felt that this stance was unpatriotic. Crystal Eastman explains why the women formed a separate peace party.

WHY A WOMAN'S Peace Party?, I am often asked. Is peace any more a concern of women than of men? Is it not of universal human concern? For a feminist—one who believes in breaking down sex barriers so that women and men can work and play and build the world together—it is not an easy question to answer. Yet the answer, when I finally worked it out in my own mind, convinced me that we should be proud and glad, even as feminists, to work for the Woman's Peace Party.

To begin with, there is a great and unique tradition behind our movement which would be lost if we merged our Woman's Peace Party in the general revolutionary international movement of the time. Do not forget that it was women who gathered at The Hague, a thousand strong, in the early months of the war, women from all the great belligerent and neutral countries, who conferred there together in friendship and sorrow and sanity while the mad war raged around them. Their great conference, despite its soundness and constructive statesmanship, failed of its purpose, failed of its hope. But from the beginning of the war down to the Russo-German armistice there was no world step of such daring and directness, nor of such honest, unfaltering international spirt and purpose, as the organization of the International Commitee of Women for Permanent Peace at The Hague in April, 1915. This Committee has branches in twenty-two countries. The Woman's Peace Party is the American section of the committee.

When the great peace conference comes, a Congress of Women made up of groups from these twenty-two countries will meet in the same city to demand that the deliberate intelligent organization of the world for lasting peace shall be the outcome of that conference.

These established international connections make it important to keep this a woman's movement.

But there is an added reason. We women of New York
State, politically speaking, have just been born. We have
been born into a world at war, and this fact cannot fail to
color greatly the whole field of our political thinking and
to determine largely the emphasis of our political action.
What we hope, then, to accomplish by keeping our movement
distinct is to bring thousands upon thousands of women
—women of the international mind—to dedicate their new
political power, not to local reforms or personal ambitions,
not to discovering the difference between the Democratic
and Republican parties, but to *ridding the world of war.*

In 1919 Jane Addams was elected president of the
Women's International League for Peace and Freedom,
a group pledged to strengthen cooperation among
women of all nations toward the goal of peace. The
group is still in existence today.

He Tore the Banner Down

The struggle for social reform once more highlighted
the importance of the vote for women. Bringing about
change in the United States ultimately required new
laws on the state and federal level. But women could
not influence lawmakers without the vote. Their lack
of political power weakened all other efforts, and so

women continued their battle to get the vote.

In 1910 Alice Paul and Lucy Burns returned from England, where they had participated in the English suffragist campaign. Fed up with petitions, the English suffragists paraded in the streets, disrupted public meetings, and even provoked violence to bring their cause to public attention. Many American suffragists feared such militancy would anger the public, most of whom wanted the suffragists to "act like ladies."

Paul and Burns formed a new organization, the Congressional Union, which worked exclusively for a federal suffrage amendment. They launched a weekly publication, *The Suffragist*. They took to the streets just as the English suffragists had, to bring the fact of women's disenfranchisement to public view. In January 1917 they organized a parade in Washington, D.C. Angry spectators disrupted their peaceful march, and troops were called in to restore order. The suffragists then started silent picketing every day at the White House entrance. They sent petitions for a federal amendment to Congress. In May, for the first time in twenty-six years, the suffrage amendment was debated in Congress.

On August 14, eight months after they had started their picketing at the White House, the suffragists unfurled a new banner. It was the time of the First

President Wilson Says, "Godspeed to the Cause"

World War; the country was now at war with Germany. The banner accused President Woodrow Wilson of being sympathetic to the Germans who did not have the privileges of democracy, but unsympathetic to American women who did not have the vote. Suffragist

Inez Haynes Irwin describes what happened after the suffragists unfurled the critical banner.

FOR A HALF an hour people gathered about the banner. The crowd grew and grew. You felt there was something brewing in them, but what, you could not guess. Suddenly it came—a man dashed from the crowd and tore the banner down. Immediately, one after another, the other banners were torn down. As fast as this happened, the banner bearers went back to Headquarters; returned with [other banners and] took up their stations again. Finally the whole line of pickets, bannerless by this time, marched back to Headquarters. The crowd, which was fast changing into a mob, followed us into Madison Place. As the pickets emerged again, the mob jumped them at the very doors of Cameron House, tore their banners away from them and destroyed them. By this time the mob, which had become a solid mass of people, choking the streets and filling the park, had evolved a leader, a yeoman [petty officer in the Navy] in uniform, who incited everybody about him to further work of destruction. Suddenly, as if by magic, a ladder appeared in their midst. A yeoman placed it against Cameron House, and accompanied by a little boy, he started up. He pulled down the [banner] of the Woman's Party which hung over the door.

Another member of the crowd climbed up the balcony and pulled down the American flag which hung beside the [banner]. Immediately Virginia Arnold and Lucy Burns appeared on the balcony carrying, the one the Kaiser banner and the other the [Women's Party] banner. The crowd began to throw eggs, tomatoes, and apples at them, but [they] stood absolutely moveless, holding the [banner].

Suddenly a shot rang out from the crowd. A bullet went through a window of the second story, directly over the heads of two women; and imbedded itself in the ceiling of the hall. The only man seen to have a revolver was a yeoman in uniform, who immediately ran up the street. Three yeomen climbed up onto the balcony and wrested the banners from the girls. As one of these men climbed over the railing, he struck Georgiana Sturgess. "Why did you do that?" she demanded, dumbfounded. The man paused a moment, apparently as amazed as she. "I don't know," he answered; then he tore the banner out of her hands and descended the ladder. Lucy Burns held her banner until the last moment. It seemed as though she were going to be dragged over the railing of the balcony, but two of the yeoman managed to tear it from her hands before this occurred. New banners were brought to replace those that had disappeared.

The suffragists tried five more times to take their banners to the White House, but angry mobs kept them away. Twenty-two banners and fourteen party flags were destroyed. The picketing and the arrests continued. On November 14 sixteen suffragists were arrested for "obstructing traffic" and sentenced to a workhouse near the capital. Once there they refused to answer any questions and insisted on talking to the superintendent of the workhouse.

SUDDENLY THE DOOR burst open, and Superintendent Whittaker came rushing in, followed by men—more and more of them. The Suffragists had been sitting or lying on the floor. Mrs. Lewis stood up.

"We demand to be treated as political pris—" she began. But that was as far as she got.

"You shut up! I have men here glad to handle you!" Whittaker said. "Seize her!"

Two men seized Mrs. Lewis, dragged her out of the sight of the remaining Suffragists.

In the meantime, another man sprang at Mrs. Nolan, who was over seventy years old, very frail and lame. [He dragged her] down the steps and away into the dark.

As Mrs. Nolan entered the hall, a man, brandishing a stick, called, "Damn you! Get in there!" [Then] two men brought in Dorothy Day—a very slight, delicate girl; her captors were twisting her arms above her head. Suddenly they lifted her, brought her body down twice over the back of an iron bench. One of the men called: "The damned Suffrager! My mother ain't no Suffrager! I will put you through hell!" Then Mrs. Nolan's captors pulled her down a corridor which opened out of this room, and pushed her through the door.

Back of Mrs. Nolan, dragged along in the same way, came Mrs. Cosu. They had been [in the cell] but a few minutes when Mrs. Lewis, all doubled over like a sack of flour, was thrown in. Her head struck the iron bed, and she fell to the floor senseless.

The other women thought she was dead. They wept over her.

Ultimately, they revived Mrs. Lewis, but Mrs. Cosu was desperately ill all night, with a heart attack and vomiting. They were afraid that she was dying, and they called at intervals for a doctor, but although there was a woman and a man guard in the corridor, they paid no attention. There were two mattresses and two blankets for the three, but that was not enough, and they shivered all night long.

In the meantime, Lucy Burns, fighting desperately all the way, had been deposited in a cell opposite. [She] began calling the roll one name after another, to see if all were there and alive. The guards called, "Shut up!" but she paid no more attention to them than if they had not spoken. "Where is Mrs. Lewis?" she demanded. Mrs. Cosu answered: "They have just thrown her in here." The guard yelled to them that if they spoke again, he would put them in strait-jackets. Mrs. Nolan and Mrs. Cosu were so terrified that they kept still for a while.

But Lucy Burns went right on calling the roll. When she refused—at the guard's order—to stop this, they hand-cuffed her wrists and fastened the handcuffs above her head to the cell door. They threatened her with a buckle gag. Little Julia Emory could do nothing to help, of course, but she put her hands above her head in exactly the same position and stood before her door until they released Lucy Burns. Lucy Burns wore her handcuffs all night.

The women were kept incommunicado and were not allowed visitors, not even their lawyer. Sixteen women went on a hunger strike as a protest against being illegally arrested and not being treated as political prisoners. Burns and Lewis were force-fed. The suffragists managed to get news of how they were being treated out of the workhouse, hoping that public knowledge of their mistreatment would pressure the government to consider the suffrage amendment. A judge ruled that their incarceration was illegal and freed them on parole. Some suffragists refused to accept the offer and were taken back to jail to finish their sentence.

These militant tactics were only one of the reasons for the passage of the nineteenth amendment giving women the vote in 1919. The National Woman Suffrage Association, under the leadership of Carrie Chapman Catt, pursued a state-by-state campaign to get women the vote. As the victories piled up, President Woodrow Wilson felt the increasing pressure to support a woman suffrage amendment, as did Congress to pass it.

In 1920, after ratification by two thirds of the states, the fifty-year battle for suffrage was over but Alice Paul's agenda for equality wasn't. She organized the National Woman's Party (NWP) to campaign for an equal rights amendment for women. Women trade unionists and most women's groups objected to the amendment. They had fought hard to get protective labor laws for women workers and felt that if an ERA passed, women would again be mistreated and abused. Paul argued the law would benefit men and women. The opponents bitterly disagreed. The amendment was voted down in Congress in 1923. It was not until 1973 that the ERA was finally approved by the Congress; it did not become law, falling three votes short for ratification.

PART SIX

RACE AND ETHNICITY

True Chivalry Respects All Womanhood

As America expanded, women of color continued to bear the double burden of racism and sexism. Long after the Civil War black women were politically and socially discriminated against because of their color and also because they were female. Shortly after Northern troops were withdrawn from the South in 1877, whites set out to intimidate blacks and to create a segregated society. Ida B. Wells, one of a growing number of black southern professionals, experienced Reconstruction's failure to equalize opportunities for blacks and saw the gradual erosion of her people's hard-won liberty.

Wells fought against the growth of Jim Crow laws—

laws promoting segregation by race on public transportation and in schools, public facilities, and restaurants. In 1888 the eighteen-year-old schoolteacher brought a lawsuit against the Ohio Railroad for trying to move her to a "colored only" part of the train. She won the suit, but lost in a higher court. Nine years later the U.S. Supreme Court, in the case of *Plessy vs. Ferguson*, declared that segregation on railroads was constitutional as long as the separate cars for blacks were equal to those for whites. The idea of "separate but equal" became the justification for segregation, which became entrenched in southern life.

In 1891 Wells protested against Memphis' inferior black schools by writing articles in the city's black-owned newspaper. She was promptly fired by the all-white School Board. She became a full-time journalist and co-owner of the Memphis *Free Speech*.

Wells watched helplessly as Southern states imposed poll taxes—payments required before one could vote—and qualifying tests that kept black men from voting. In addition to these devices created to intimidate blacks, southern racists terrorized blacks with beatings and lynchings.

Black women, regardless of their economic position or educational level, knew their husbands, fiancés, brothers, and fathers were never safe. Their men could be taken from their homes and murdered at whim at any time. Black women were also vulnerable to attack; they continued to be sexually exploited by white men just as they had been during slavery. There was no legal recourse if they were raped, for no southern court would believe the claims of a black woman over those of a white man.

In March 1892 three highly respected black businessmen in Memphis were lynched. The black population was outraged and horrified. At that time the most common excuse given for lynching was that white women had to be protected from the lust of black men. Wells challenged this lie and charged that the lynching occurred because the three black men were taking business away from a white man. She investigated other lynchings and found that most rape charges were false. The truth was the reverse—while black men did not rape white women, black women were habitually raped and otherwise sexually abused by white men. Wells insisted that lynching was part of a carefully orchestrated plan to keep blacks in their place, to frighten them from voting, running for public office, or operating successful businesses, and to keep them from trying to achieve their equal place in society.

In May 1892, when Wells was out of town, the white community responded to her editorials by de-

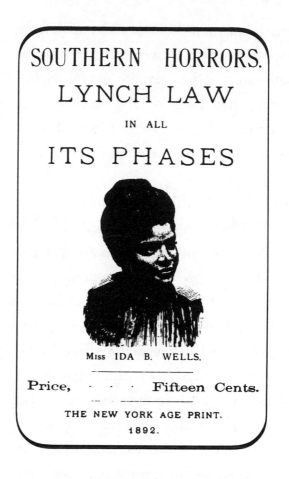

stroying her newspaper office. Wells never returned to Memphis but carried her antilynching crusade across the United States and into Europe. In this excerpt from her book *A Red Record*, she attacks the myth that black men rape white women and brings up the explosive question of voluntary relationships between white women and black men.

NOT ALL OR nearly all of the murders done by white men, during the past thirty years in the South, have come to light, but the statistics as gathered and preserved by white men, and which have not been questioned, show that during these years more than ten thousand Negroes have been killed in cold blood, without the formality of judicial trial and legal execution. As yet, as evidence of the absolute impunity with which the white man dares to kill a Negro, the same record shows that during all these years, and for all these murders only three white men have been tried, convicted, and executed.

If the Southern people in defense of their lawlessness, would tell the truth and admit that colored men and women are lynched for almost any offense, from murder to a misdemeanor, there would not now be the necessity for [the defense that Negroes had to be killed to avenge their assaults upon white women]. But when they intentionally, maliciously and constantly belie the record and bolster up these falsehoods by the words of legislators, preachers, governors and bishops, then the Negro must give to the world his side of the awful story.

The question must be asked, what the white man means when he charges the black man with rape. Does he mean the crime which the statutes of the states describe as such? Not by any means. The Southern white man says that it is impossible for a voluntary alliance to exist between a white woman and a colored man, and therefore, the fact of an alliance is a proof of force. In numerous instances where colored men have been lynched on the charge of rape, it was positively known at the time of lynching, and indisputably proven after the victim's death, that the relationship sustained between the man and the woman was voluntary and clandestine, and that in no court of law could even the charge of assault have been successfully maintained.

It was for the assertion of this fact, in the defense of her own race, that the writer hereof became an exile; her property destroyed and her return to her home forbidden under penalty of death, for writing the following editorial which was printed in her paper, the *Free Speech*, in Memphis, Tenn., May 21, 1892:

Nobody in this section of the country believes the old threadbare lie that Negro men rape white women. If Southern white men are not careful, they will over-reach themselves and public sentiment will have a reaction; a conclusion will then be reached which will be very damaging to the moral reputation of their women."

It is not the purpose of this defense to say one word against the white women of the South. Such need not be said, but it is their misfortune that the white men of that section to justify their own barbarism assume a chivalry which they do not possess. True chivalry respects all womanhood, and no one who reads the record, as it is written in the faces of the million mulattoes in the South, will for a minute conceive that the southern white man had a very chivalrous regard for the honor due the women of his race or respect for the womanhood which circumstances placed in his power.

I Cannot Believe that This Is Superstitious Reverence

As settlers moved west, Indians were forced off their lands and coerced onto reservations. Federal treaties, guaranteeing money and land to the Indians, were continually broken.

By the late nineteenth century most Native American women, whose people had lived in North America for thousands of years before the arrival of Europeans, found their world constricted to the reservation. Their lives were largely defined by federal and state governments.

Lyda B. Conley was a descendant of the Wyandotte tribe. Little else is known about her background. In the early twentieth century she was a lawyer in Missouri, an unusual accomplishment for any woman. Conley probably attended a federally run boarding school off the reservation and then went on to college and law school or clerked in some willing lawyer's office. A photograph of Conley in a frilly white dress and flowered hat indicates that she had adopted some of the ways of white society, but Conley did not forget her heritage and dedicated her life to fighting against white society's mistreatment of Indians.

In 1904 Conley learned that Kansas City business-men wanted to raze the cemetery where her mother

Lyda B. Conley

and other members of the Wyandotte tribe were buried. The businessmen planned to develop the area as part of the city's commercial district; her ancestors' bodies were to be moved to another cemetery. To Wyandottes and other Indian peoples (and to many whites and other peoples), disturbing the bones and spirits of their ancestors is an outrageous act of desecration. When Indian people die, their remains must never be disturbed or displaced. Lyda and her sister Helene

(Floating Voice) were outraged that this sacred site, ceded to their people by the U.S. government as a burial place "in perpetuity," was being destroyed.

Conley and her sister devised a plan to stop the desecration of the cemetery: In the middle of the night, the sisters snuck into it and built a six-by-eight-foot wooden shack on the grounds. For the next six years, despite federal orders to remove the dead bodies and attempted work by contractors, the sisters refused to budge from the shack. While serving guard duty in the shack, Lyda prepared her legal case and studied for the Kansas bar so she could appear before the state court. When the state court rejected her request to stop the razing, she appealed to the United States Supreme Court. In her Supreme Court brief, she traces the history of the federal government's legal obligations to her people and compares her people's "superstitious reverence" about burial with the concerns of the Bible's Old Testament patriarchs.

LIKE JACOB OF old [who asked his sons to bury him with his fathers] I too, when I shall be gathered unto my people, desire that they bury me with my fathers in Huron Cemetery, the most sacred and hallowed spot on earth to me, and I cannot believe that this is superstitious reverence any more than I can believe that the reverence every true American has for the grave of Washington at Mount Vernon is a superstitious reverence.

Huron Cemetery is known to be the oldest burial ground in the State of Kansas. Just when the first interment was made therein, we have not been able to ascertain. We find however, that in the year 1843, a chief by the name of Matthew Peacock, aged 68 years, and in the year 1844, Squeendechtee, another chief who was at that time 61 years of age, died and was buried therein. Other chiefs whose graves we find there are Rontondo or Warpole, Tauromee, Sommodwat, Hawdownwaugh or Matthews, Monocue or Thomas, Dawatout or John Hicks, Big Tree, Tall Charles, Sarahoss, Clark Armstrong and many others space will not permit us to mention.

The wisest man the world has ever known admonishes "Remove not the ancient [landmark], which thy fathers have set." And that the hand of the desecrator "Remove not the old landmark; and enter not unto the fields of the fatherless": "For their redeemer is mighty; he shall plead their cause with thee."

Man goeth to his long home, and the mourners go about the streets: or ever the silver cord be loose, or the golden bowl be broken, or the pitcher be broken at the fountain, or the wheel broken at the cistern.

Then shall the dust return to the earth as it was: and spirit shall return unto God who gave it.

The Supreme Court did not agree with Conley's arguments. Women's clubs rallied to her cause and brought wider public sentiment against destroying the cemetery. In 1912 the Indians Affairs Committee of the U.S. House of Representatives supported a bill forbidding the cemetery's sale. Lyda B. Conley was buried along with her ancestors in Huron Cemetery on May 28, 1946.

Outfitted with Western Clothing

The overwhelming majority of immigrants coming to the United States from 1880 to 1914 were from eastern and southern Europe. American prejudice, reflected in its immigration policy, had always made it difficult for Asians to immigrate. At the turn of the century Japanese women began immigrating to the United States, but in 1924 legislation barred all immigrants from Asia. Japanese women, among others, could not join their husbands and many Japanese American men were deprived of the opportunity of marrying Japanese women.

During the time that Japanese women were allowed to immigrate to the United States, most arrived as brides through arranged marriages, a long-standing Japanese tradition. Some women joined their husbands, who had gone ahead and were already settled in America. Others left their friends and families to settle in a strange country with men they had not yet met. Leaving home meant losing the emotional and economic support of family and friends, and facing the uncertainty of life in America. These uncertainties were heightened by the cultural differences between Japanese life and life in the United States.

The journey across the sea was made somewhat bearable by being with other women in similar circumstances. Arrival meant getting past immigration officials, none of whom spoke Japanese. Some unlucky women were detained because of suspected diseases. Once past immigration, the women were usually outfitted in Western clothes. The Japanese, aware that Chinese immigrants had been excluded in 1882, thought that Western clothing would make them and their wives less vulnerable to the charge that they, like the Chinese, were not easily assimilated into American life.

There was rarely time or money for a celebration of the marriage, or of the reunion of husband and wife. Women who stayed in the city went immediately to work in laundries. Those who went to rural areas worked long hours in the fields and were responsible for all the housework as well. Four different Japanese women describe their new life in America.

I LEFT YOKOHAMA on the *Minnesota*. Passengers from Yo-kohama were placed into rooms partitioned by canvas. Besides myself and two other married women returning to America, there was a couple. The two married women had left their children in Japan and would cry when they talked about them. I, too, broke out in tears when I thought of my father, who had passed away before my departure.

~

I was immediately outfitted with Western clothing at Hara's Clothing Store. Because I had to wear a tight corset around my chest, I could not bend forward. I had to have my husband tie my shoe laces. There were some women who fainted because it was too tight. There are stories of women being carried to the hotel rooms by their husband who hurriedly untied the corset strings which were not joking matters. In my case, I wore a large hat, a high-necked blouse, a long skirt, a buckled belt around my waist, high-laced shoes, and of course, for the first time in my life, a brassiere and hip pads.

~

At the beginning I worked with my husband picking potatoes or onions and putting them in sacks. Working with rough-and-tumble men, I became weary to the bones; waking up in the mornings I could not bend over the wash basin. Sunlight came out about 4:00 A.M. during the summer in the Yakima Valley. I arose at 4:30. After cooking breakfast, I went out to the fields. There was no electric stove or gas like now. It took over one hour to cook, burning kindling wood. As soon as I came home, I first put on the fire, took off my hat, and then I washed my hands. After cooking both breakfast and lunch, I went to the fields.

~

My husband did not think of helping in the house or with the children. No matter how busy I may have been, he never changed the baby's diapers. Though it may not be right to say this ourselves, we Issei [immigrant Japanese] pioneer women from Japan worked solely for our husbands. At mealtime, whenever there was not enough food, we served a lot to our husbands and took very little for ourselves.

A Girl Without a Cent to Her Name

The custom of "arranged" marriages crossed the ocean with Eastern European immigrants as well. Many young women found themselves caught in the clash between the traditional ethnic customs and the new society in which immigrants struggled to establish themselves. The arranged marriage of Rahel Cohen is one example of this. Cohen, a Russian Jew, immigrated to New York City around 1900. When she was sixteen, her parents found her a "very desirable" young man who owned a grocery. She understood that this arranged marriage would free her from her dismal life as a shirtwaist worker and provide financial security for her and her parents as well. She agreed to meet the suitor.

FATHER WAS SO pleased at the news [that the suitor's family found me acceptable] that his face became quite radiant.

"A girl without a cent to her name," he said, quite lost in wonder. Mother too looked pleased.

"And what do you say, Rahel?" [father] asked.

Somehow I had never quite realised that this question would really be put to me and that I would have to answer it. "Well," father said in an easy tone, as if he were quite sure of the outcome, "there is plenty of time. Think it over."

When [the next day] father asked me, "Well, what do you say?" I trembled. "I have not decided yet," I told him quietly.

"Do you want to see him again?" he asked.

I said: "No."

He thought for a moment. "I don't see what you want," he said. "He is a nice quiet young man and the main thing, he is not a wage earner. The smallest business man is worth ten workingmen. Tell me definitely to-morrow night. We cannot keep the people waiting for an answer any longer. This is not child's play, you know." When father was out of hearing mother added sadly, by way of help perhaps, "It is true that you are young, but you see, father is poor and you are not strong!"

I went into the bedroom and wept with my face buried in the pilows.

"Father is poor and I am not strong." These words had impressed themselves in my mind.

"It is clear then," I thought [a day later], "that I must marry. And if I did not marry this young man whom could I marry? A tailor?" At the thought of a tailor the young man rose in my estimation. I also saw an advantage in that he was a grocer. "My people could live near and get things at cost price, bread, butter, sugar, potatoes. I will be a great help." But on the other hand I could not picture myself living with the strange young man and his mother. I knew now that he had a mother; she was blind. He was her only son and she would live with him then as now.

It struck me how similar my fate was to my mother's. She too had married an only son, and his mother had been blind. If I did not marry this young man, what then?

"Well," [my father] asked, "what have you decided?" It grew so still, even the breathing seemed to have stopped. And in this stillness, I heard myself say, "Yes."

I did not look up. I knew that every face had grown brighter. It was pleasant to know I was the cause. I had been nothing but a sorrow for so long.

[On] Friday Israel came to our house about seven o'clock and showed us two little tickets which were still unfamiliar to my family and myself. "These are for the theatre," he said, "for to-night." We walked to the theatre in silence. This was the second time I was out alone with him. The first time had been when we went to get the ring. Then, I merely felt awkward when walking with him. But now I felt nervous and miserable. The silence oppressed me and as we walked along, his sleeve, as if by design, kept coming in contact with mine, and I kept edging away, but very slowly so as not to hurt his feelings. In our seats in the balcony it was the same way. He was very attentive but chiefly with looks, and his elbow was on the arm of my seat. I pressed into the farthest corner and could think of nothing but how to keep clear.

The walk home was again a silent one. I said good night and turned to go when he called "Rahel!" His voice sounded so muffled. He came and stood near me. "I want one kiss," he said. I felt panic-stricken.

"Oh, I couldn't!" I said, "I couldn't possibly. Indeed I couldn't!"

"But, we are engaged now," he said in a hurt tone as if he felt he were within his rights. It flashed through my mind what married life may mean with a person for whom one does not care. "I couldn't possibly. I am sorry."

[In the morning I told mother] that I could not marry Israel. I clung to her and begged her not to blame me. She spoke tenderly and tried to quiet me. The children gathered around the couch and father came in. I expected he would upbraid me. But he was as tender as mother who stood with her arms tight around me. "Hush! hush!" he said, "if you feel so unhappy you need not marry him."

"And won't I be forced?" I asked.

"You won't be forced."

"Can no one force me?"

There were tears in his eyes. "No one can force you."

Still I kept asking it over and over again and laughed and cried hysterically.

They Will Not Listen to Their Mother

Every aspect of immigrants' lives in the New World challenged their traditions and beliefs. The surroundings, work conditions, and living arrangements were very different from any immigrant's previous life. Old World patterns of relationships between men and women and between women and their children were constantly challenged. Adjustment was painful, and for some impossible.

Around 1904 Helena Brylska emigrated to the United States from a small village in Poland, leaving her children behind until she had found a new home. She settled in Union City, Connecticut, where she worked in a factory. By 1907, having saved enough money to have her children brought over, she wrote to her sister to send them. Her subsequent letters reveal the new powerlessness she felt over her family, and the pain, and anger she felt from her weakened maternal authority. The security of the extended family, which helped define her maternal role in Poland, did not operate in America, where the married couple was more isolated. Competing factors such as school and peers challenged the old alliances to the family.

April 19 [1907?]

Dear Sister:

You write, dear sister, that Józiek is ill with his eyes. It would be very painful for me if you should not send him, dear sister. And [their step]father would be terribly angry and terribly grieved, if they all may not come. So I beg you very much, sister dear, send him. If he does not come

Immigrant mother and children

it will be a terrible sorrow and trial for us, and a large
expense, because they will not give us the money for the
ship ticket back; and I shall bear a grief in my heart, that
I endeavored to have this child and have it not. Remember,
dear sister, send him to me, I beg you for the love [of
God?]. And now you wrote that you will send me a shawl,
but don't make any trouble about it for yourself, and for
the [man] who comes. May only my children come; I don't

wish anything more. As you grieve about your children, so
I grieve about mine. And I beg you once more, send me
all the children, because the ship tickets are sent for all of
them in order that they may all come. We salute you all
and we wish you every good. Both of us beg for all the
children.

> Dąbrowskis
> [Helena Brylska's married name]

June 6 [1908?]

Dear Sister,

I write as to a sister and I complain as to a sister about
my children from the old country—those three boys. I did
not have them with me, and I grieved continuously about
them; and today again, on the other hand, my heart is
bleeding. They will not listen to their mother. If they would
listen, they would do well with me. But no, they wish only
to run everywhere about the world, and I am ashamed before
people that they are so bad. They arrived, I sent them to
school, because it is obligatory to send them; if you don't
do it the teacher comes and takes them by the collar. So
they have been going, but the oldest was annoyed with the
school: "No, mama, I will go to work." I say, "Go on to
school." But "No!" and "No!" Without certificates from
the school they won't let them work. I got certificates for
the two oldest ones: "Go, if you wish." They worked for
some time, but they got tired of work. One went with a
Jew to ramble about corners [trading or amusing himself?],
and for some days was not to be seen; I had to go and to
search for him. The worst one of them is Stach; the two

others are a little better. They were good in the beginning but now they know how to speak English, and their goodness is lost. I have no comfort at all. I complain [to you] as a sister, perhaps you will relieve me at least with a letter, if you write me some words, dear sister. We remain, well-wishing,

H. J. Dąbrowskis

April 5 [1910 or 1911]

As to the children, two of them are very good children. One is working and gives his money [to me], the other is going to school and learns well, but the third is not at home at all. Stach has been bad, is bad, and will be bad. So long as he was smaller, he remained more at home. I begged him, "Stach, remain at home with your mother." No, he runs away and loafs about. Well let him run. I had his eyes wiped [had him instructed] as well as I could; he can read, write, and speak English, quite like a gentleman. You say, "Beat." In America you are not allowed to beat; they can put you into a prison. Give them to eat, and don't beat—such is the law in America. Nothing can be done and you advise to beat! Nothing can be done; if he is not good of himself, he is lost.

I regret that I took the children from our country so soon. In our country perhaps they would have had some misery, and in America they have none, and because of this many become dissolute. In America children have a good life; they don't go to any pastures, but to school, and that is their whole work.

H. J. Dąbrowskis

PART SEVEN

THE MODERN WOMAN

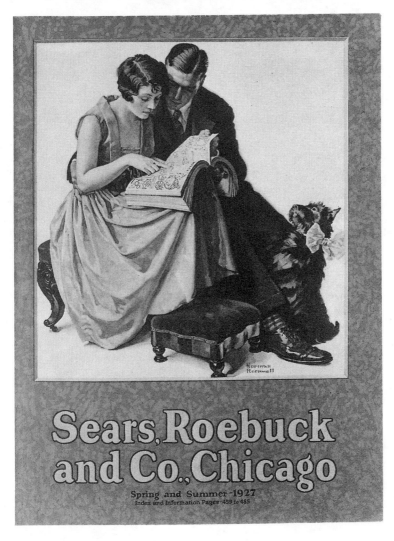

Sears, Roebuck and Co., Chicago

Spring and Summer-1927

Index and Information Pages-459 to 485

Dear Mrs. Sanger

All American women faced the same dilemma of how to control their reproductive lives—how to avoid unwanted pregnancies. Information on contraception and contraceptive devices had been available in the 1830s but not widely used. In 1873, with the passage of the Comstock Laws, information about contraception and the manufacturing, selling, and advertising of contraceptive devices was considered "obscene." Anyone mailing or receiving "obscene" material could be fined or imprisoned. Better-educated, well-to-do women might find ways around the laws and obtain birth control methods. But more often women avoided pregnancy by limiting sex to when they desired children. Some women abstained from sex as much as possible. Many women who had unwanted pregnancies damaged themselves or killed themselves by self-induced abortions.

Margaret Sanger, a public-health nurse in New York's lower east side in 1912, saw how disastrous life was for women who did not have control over their reproductive lives. Her poor patients were constantly pregnant, overburdened from childbearing and child rearing, worn out by bearing as many as ten children by the time they were forty. For forty years Sanger helped women by providing them with information and safe, effective birth control methods. She was harassed, jailed, and brought to trial, but this didn't stop her from opening birth-control clinics or writing books that helped free women from "enforced motherhood." Women in towns and cities across the nation, wanting to experience their own sexuality without becoming pregnant, wrote to Sanger for her help. Here are three of the thousands of letters she received.

Wisconsin, May 5, 1921.

Dear Madam:

Have read your book *Women and the New Race*, and am more than interested in its contents. I think it's just wonderful. It expresses everything that many women have felt, but never dared breathe. I have been married seventeen years and have had mostly all the troubles the majority of married women have, have four living children, had one miscarriage and eight abortions. No doubt you will think it almost

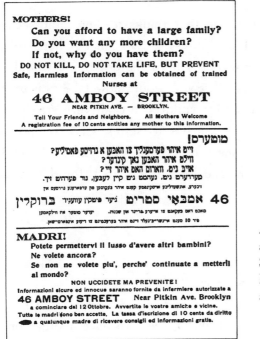

A 1916 handbill advertising Margaret Sanger's clinic in English, Yiddish, and Italian

unbelievable, but nevertheless it's true, and true only because I'm ignorant in these things as most women are, so I come to you for advice. Please tell me what a contraceptive is, and where to get such. It will be a blessing to me, and I will bless you to the end of my days.

Sincerely yours,
Mrs. R. S.

Minnesota, May 20, 1921.

Dear Mrs. Sanger:

I would like to ask you to help me as soon as you can. I am a mother of 11 children, 10 living. Green, that is what I am, only 34 years old and am 3 months in a family way again. I have a man that thinks it's my fault because we have children. I do confess it is. I am out here on the farm, no money or way to get to the doctors. I would not care how I would get threw. I would now take poison, for I do hate life again. Our children are all very strong and healthy, but I am the one has to suffer. Can you not tell me or help me in some way. I have a daughter 17 and 15. I want them to know and be better than I, for this is sure hell.

Mrs. S. J.

Minnesota

Dear Mrs. M. H. Sanger:

I am a married woman and got 3 children, two boys and one girl, and I feel like if I was to have another one I would rather die. The first one was a boy and I was helpless all the time while I carried him, and was sick for (20) twenty hours. When he was born the Dr. didn't expect him to live but he came through alright anyhow. The next was a girl, which was born (2) two months too early. I worried and worked so hard till I became so nervous and weak, but I saved her just the same. She is 3 years now, and is getting quite strong so I hope I can save her. The last one is also a boy, weight 11 lbs when born. While I carried him I was weak all the time. I would fall down lots of time while doing my house work, and then I would lay on the floor till my husband would come home and pick me up and put me to bed, so I think I sure have had my share of having children. I love them all with all my heart, but we are poor only working for a living and I think its more sin to bring children into this world and let them go half dressed and half starved. I worried so since this high cost of living came on and no work for a man to do, that I often think we all would be better off dead, but I hope you will send me the way of keeping out of having any more children.

Please send soon to

Mrs. W. N.

Extraordinarily Free

During World War I (1914–18) women were given the opportunity to work in jobs previously held by men. Though they lost these jobs when the men returned home, they had tasted freedom and independence, and liked it. By 1920 changes in marital laws, new ideas of sexual liberation, availability of birth control devices, and opportunities for college education greatly expanded the options of middle-class women. Mass-produced goods freed them from some housework. They could buy factory-made clothes for their families instead of sewing them. They bought canned and baked goods instead of doing all the cooking and baking themselves. Oil furnaces, indoor running water, vacuum cleaners, electric irons had also simplified housework. The new mass communications of the radio and women's magazines contained advertising

that campaigned to get women to buy the newest
and best of everything—household appliances, cosmet-
ics, and the latest fashions. The number of women
graduating from high school and college increased
dramatically. More women entered college and the
professions despite continuing sex discrimination in
the fields of ministry, medicine, and law. Poorer women,
such as those who wrote to Margaret Sanger, struggled
to control the basic terms of their existence.

Margaret Mead, who became one of the world's
most prominent anthropologists, was one of this new
generation of middle-class women who felt free to
define their lives as they wanted to. Mead and her
friends did not accept the rules of others concerning
what careers were appropriate for them because they
were women, or whom they should marry, or how
and when to have children. They saw problems as
challenges to be solved. Unlike most nineteenth-
century feminists, who saw no way to combine marriage
and career, Mead and her friends expected to have
both if they wanted them. They demanded the same
compatibility and companionship with their male mates
as they had with their women friends. If a relationship
with a man didn't work out, they looked for another.
For them, divorce was not a stigma but an acceptable
option for failed compatibility. In these excerpts from

her autobiography, Mead describes her life from the years she was in college through her three marriages, and tells of her unexpected joy when she learned that she would be able to have a child:

WE BELONGED TO a generation of young women who felt extraordinarily free—free from the demand to marry unless we chose to do so, free to postpone marriage while we did other things, free from the need to bargain and hedge that had burdened and restricted women of earlier generations. We laughed at the idea that a woman could be an old maid at the age of twenty-five, and we rejoiced at the new medical care that made it possible for a woman to have a child at forty.

We firmly established a style of relationships to other women. "Never break a date with a girl for a man" was one of our mottoes in a period when women's loyalty to women usually was—as it usually still is—subordinate to their possible relationships to men. We learned loyalty to women, pleasure in conversation with women, and enjoyment of the way in which we complemented one another in terms of our differences in temperament, which we found as interesting as the complementarity that is produced by the difference of sex.

As a girl, I knew that someday I would have children. My closest models, my mother and my grandmother, had both had children and also had used their minds and had careers in the public world. So I had no doubt that, whatever career I might choose, I would have children, too.

In the 1920s, we believed that children should be wanted and planned for. We were all very conscious of the new possibilities of birth control and safer childbirth, which mean that one could have a child even late in life. Luther and I wanted to finish our graduate work before we had a child, and then my field trip and Luther's traveling fellowship in Europe meant another postponement. But I was so sure that we would have children that advice that I would do better to stay at home and have a child than to go off to Samoa to study adolescent girls seemed peculiar to me. After all, men were not told to give up field work to have children! And I felt, rather than knew, that postponement —even postponement for a whole lifetime—need do no harm.

And then, in 1926, when I was told that I could never have children, I took this as a kind of omen about my future. I had married Luther with the hope of rearing a houseful of children in the country parish. But now he was giving up the ministry and I was told that I could not have a child. I believed he would make a wonderful father, but this was no longer a possibility—for us.

On the other hand, I did not think that Reo, who wanted to marry me, would make an ideal father. He was too demanding and jealous of my attention; he begrudged even the attention I gave to a piece of mending. I had always felt that my father demanded too much of my mother and took her away from us to satisfy his own immediate and capricious requests to do something or find something for him. I did not want a marriage that repeated this pattern.

But without children, the future looked quite different, and I decided to choose a life of shared field work and intellectual endeavor. I do not remember being terribly disappointed. There had always been the alternative of another kind of life.

Later, when Gregory [Mead's third husband] and I were married, I continued to hope for a child, but once again I had several early miscarriages.

From the moment it was certain that I was pregnant, I took extreme precautions [and] kept the baby.

[My next problem was around the birth and how to] cope with all the tiresome regulations of hospitals and doctors that made breast feeding difficult and prevented a mother from keeping the baby in the room with her.

I decided to start with the coming baby and work backward. I [found] Ben Spock, a young pediatrician. I explained to Ben that I wanted him to be present at the birth, so that he could take over the baby's care immediately, that I wanted to have a film made of the baby's birth, so that afterward it could be referred to with some degree of accuracy; that I wanted a wet nurse if my milk was slow in coming in, and that I wanted permission to adjust the feeding schedule to the baby instead of the clock.

Ben replied genially that he would come to the delivery and that I could feed the baby as often as I pleased.

During these months [of pregnancy] I had all the familiar apprehensions about what the baby would be like. I schooled myself not to hope for a boy or a girl, but to keep an open mind. I schooled myself to have no image of what the child would look like and no expectations about the gifts he or she might, or might not, have.

I did not, of course, have to contend with the kinds of ambivalence that bedevil the newly married, who are afraid of sharing their recently established intimacy with a new-comer. Nor did I worry about what having a child might do to my career. I already had a reputation on which I could rest for several years.

At the hospital I was made to time my own pains with an ordinary watch, and I remember my annoyance at not having a stopwatch. In the end, the baby's birth had to be slowed down for ten minutes while Myrtle McGraw, who was making the film of the birth, sent for a flashbulb that had been left in her car. I was fascinated to discover that far from being "ten times worse than the worst pain you have ever had" (as our childless woman doctor had told us at college) or "worse than the worst cramps you ever had, but at least you get something out of it" (as my mother had said), the pains of childbirth were altogether different from the enveloping effects of other kinds of pain. These were pains one could follow with one's mind; they were like a fine electric needle outlining one's pelvis.

Mary Catherine Bateson was born and looked very much herself.

30 Cents an Hour

The stock-market crash in October 1929 brought a ten-year economic depression to the United States. Unemployment rose from four and a half million people

Migrant worker harvesting tomatoes, Santa Clara Valley, California, 1938

in 1930 to thirteen million in 1933. One out of four people couldn't find a job. Hundreds of thousands of Americans were hungry and homeless. For poor people life had always been a struggle for existence, but now that struggle was intensified. For middle-class Americans, used to financial security, the Depression was a new experience, shocking and frightening them into the realization that economic change affected family and personal life. Discouraged and desperate, many men deserted their families. Couples postponed getting married, having children, or divorcing—all were too costly. The birth rate dropped as women sought out contraception at birth control clinics.

The Depression fueled the old clichés that "a woman's place is in the home" and that "the workplace is a man's domain." Many Americans believed that with such massive unemployment, married women should stay home and leave the jobs to men. They insisted it was unfair for any family to have two wage earners while other families had none. They argued that women were needed at home to "nuture" the family during this difficult time.

Government policies tried to keep women out of the labor force, too. From 1932 to 1937 federal law forbade more than one family member to work for the federal civil service. State and local governments had similar policies barring married women from government jobs. Half the state legislatures proposed bills to keep women from any jobs. Only a vigorous lobbying campaign by women's organizations defeated these bills. Married women could not be hired in 77 percent of the school systems, and those who chose to marry were often fired.

Despite these barriers women continued working and looking for work, and the number of married women wage earners grew. Under President Franklin Delano Roosevelt's New Deal, jobs opened in social service and education. More clerical workers were needed to help the government run its new programs. Women took these jobs that male workers did not want; not only were they the low-paying jobs, but they were the jobs that had long been identified as "women's" jobs.

Women also found work in factories where government loans were being used to modernize the plants. When the old machines were replaced by new, simplified procedures, women were hired to run the new machines—at lower wages than men had received before. Women's wages were lower in the garment, textile, and leather industries. The Works Progress Administration (WPA) paid male workers five dollars a day, against three dollars for women.

The New Deal programs did little to help black women, 90 percent of whom were domestics or agricultural workers, for such occupations were not protected under these programs. Mexican-American farm laborers fared just as poorly. In the first excerpt a reporter describes what life was like for northern black domestic workers in New York City. In the second selection Jessie Lopez de la Cruz describes her life as a migrant farm worker in California.

EVERY MORNING, RAIN or shine, groups of women with brown paper bags or cheap suitcases stand on street corners in the Bronx and Brooklyn waiting for a chance to get some work. Sometimes there are 15, sometimes 30, some are old, many are young and most of them are Negro women waiting for employers to come to the street corner auction blocks to bargain for their labor.

They come as early as 7 in the morning, wait as late as four in the afternoon with the hope that they will make enough to buy supper when they go home. Some have spent their last nickel to get to the corner and are in desperate need. When the hour grows late, they sit on boxes if they are around. In the afternoon their labor is worth only half as much as in the morning. If they are lucky, they get about 30 cents an hour scrubbing, cleaning, laundering, washing windows, waxing floors and woodwork all day long; in the afternoon, when most have already been employed, they are only worth the degrading sum of 20 cents an hour.

Once hired on the "slave market," the women often find after a day's backbreaking toil, that they worked longer than was arranged, got less than was promised, were forced to accept clothing instead of cash and were exploited beyond human endurance. Only the urgent need for money makes them submit to this routine daily.

Throughout the country, more than two million women are engaged in domestic work, the largest occupational group for women. About half are Negro women.

Though many Negro women work for as little as two dollars a week and as long as 80 hours a week, they have no social security, no workmen's compensation, no old age security.

~

From 1939 until 1944 we were still following the crops. We would go out to pick cotton or apricots or grapes here near Fresno or we would go farther north to Tracey to pick peas. When there was no work chopping or picking cotton we'd go to Patterson or San Jose to pick apricots.

We always went where we wanted to make sure the women and men were going to work because if it were just the men working it wasn't worth going out there because we wouldn't earn enough to support a family. We would start early, around 6:30 A.M. and work for four or five hours, then walk home and eat and rest until about three-thirty in the afternoon when it cooled off. We would go back and work until we couldn't see. Then we'd get home and rest, visit, talk, then I'd clean up the kitchen. I was doing the housework and working out in the fields, and taking care of the kids. I had two children by this time.

I used a short-handled hoe in the lettuce fields. The lettuce grows in a bed. You work in little furrows between two rows. First you thin them with the hoe, then you pick off the tops. My brothers-in-law and Arnold [her husband] and I and some other friends worked there picking the tops off the lettuce. By the time they had taken up one row I had taken up two. The men would go between the two beds and take one row and break the little balls off. But I took two rows at a time, one with each hand. By the time I finished my two rows at the other end, it was close to a mile long, and my brother-in-law had only taken one row part-way. He said, "I'm quitting! If Jessie can beat me at this kind of work, I'm not good at it." So he never came back. About three or four other men wouldn't go back to work because they were beaten by a woman. They said, "I'm ashamed to have a woman even older than I am work faster than I can. This is women's job." I said, "Hey! What do you mean? You mean the men's job is washing dishes and baking tortillas?" They said working out in the fields was women's work because we were faster at it!

Having Learned to Stare Down Fear

During the difficult years of the Depression, millions of Americans wrote to President Roosevelt and his advisors for help. And for the first time in history, women turned to a President's wife for help. Eleanor Roosevelt was an established political figure in her own right when her husband became president in 1933. She worked within the New York Democratic State Committee to establish laws limiting child labor and to enforce an eight-hour day and minimum wages for women. She was a member of the Women's Trade Union League and a friend of Rose Schneiderman's and other women reformers. She organized a White House Conference to discuss how to more effectively help unemployed women. Mrs. Roosevelt urged the President to include more women and minorities in his New Deal programs.

She also urged the President to appoint more women to government posts. Frances Perkins, the Secretary of Labor, became the first woman cabinet member. The women's project of the Federal Emergency Relief Administration was headed by Ellen Woodward, a Mississippi legislator and social reformer. Rose Schneiderman was appointed to the advisory board of the National Recovery Administration (NRA). Mary McLeod Bethune, a prominent black educator, headed programs for black youth at the National Youth Administration. Mrs. Roosevelt's activities on behalf of women and minorities prompted one reporter to comment that the White House was becoming "Hull House on Pennsylvania Avenue."

Eleanor Roosevelt's energy, concern for people, and commitment to her ideals made her a role model for millions of women around the world. In her autobiography she describes her journey from being a frightened, awkward young girl to the woman eventually called The First Lady of the World.

BECAUSE I FELT as only a young girl can feel it, all the pain of being an ugly duckling, I was not only timid, I was afraid. Afraid of almost everything, I think: of mice, of the dark, of imaginary dangers, of my own inadequacy. My chief objective, as a girl, was to do my duty. This had been drilled into me as far back as I could remember.

Not my duty as I saw it, but my duty as laid down for me by other people. It never occurred to me to revolt. Anyhow, my one overwhelming need in those days was to be approved, to be loved, and I did whatever was required of me, hoping it would bring me nearer to the approval and love I so much wanted.

As a young woman, my sense of duty remained as strict and rigid as it had been when I was a girl, but it had changed its focus. My husband and my children became the center of my life and their needs were my new duty. I am afraid now that I approached this new obligation much as I had my childhood duties. I was still timid, still afraid of doing something wrong, of making mistakes, or not living up to the standards required by my mother-in-law, of failing to do what was expected of me.

As a result, I was so hidebound by duty that I became too critical, too much of a disciplinarian. I was so concerned with bringing up my children properly that I was not wise enough just to love them. Now, looking back, I think I would rather spoil a child a little and have more fun out of it.

It was not until I reached middle age that I had the courage to develop interests of my own, outside of my duties to my family. In the beginning, it seems to me now, I had no goal beyond the interests themselves, in learning about people and conditions and the world outside our own United States. Almost at once I began to discover that interest leads to interest, knowledge leads to more knowledge, the capacity for understanding grows with the effort to understand.

From that time on, though I have had many problems, though I have known the grief and the loneliness that are the lot of most human beings, though I have had to make and still have to make endless adjustments, I have never been bored, never found the days long enough for the range of activities with which I wanted to fill them. And, having learned to stare down fear, I long ago reached the point where there is no living person whom I fear, and few challenges that I am not willing to face.

Simply Remarkable

World War II, not the New Deal, pulled America out of its economic depression and put women into jobs that had previously been closed to them. The enlistment of millions of men in the army created an emergency labor shortage. Workers were needed in defense plants and in factories producing consumer goods. Government propaganda urged women to do their patriotic duty by leaving their homes and stepping into the factories.

Over six million women who had never worked before responded. Between 1940 and 1945 the number of women working increased by 50 percent. In 1940, women made up 25 percent of the civilian work force; by 1945 that figure had risen to 36 percent. Three quarters of these new workers were married. The number of women workers in the defense industry rose 460 percent as women moved into skilled, higher-paying industrial jobs that had previously been open only to men. Women built airplanes and ships. They became toolmakers, drill press operators, steel workers, lumberjacks, welders, and train conductors. "Rosie the Riveter," pictured in newspapers and magazines, became a national symbol. Armed with her protective mask and acetylene torch, Rosie symbolized women's prowess and dispelled the myth that women could not handle physically demanding jobs.

In smaller numbers, women joined the armed forces. Over 350,000 women served with the Women's Army Corps (WAC), the Navy's WAVES, the Marine Corps Women's Reserves (MCWR), the Coast Guard's SPARS, the Army Nurse Corps (ANC) and the Navy Nurse Corps. The WACS accepted married women, but women with children under fourteen were ineligible. The WAVES and MCWR excluded those with children under eighteen. Black women were excluded from the WAVES until October 1944.

War nurses tended the wounded under fire on the battlefields. But most military women found themselves on the home front in traditional female jobs, working as typists, clerks, switchboard operators, cooks, and administrators. Black women were segregated in all-black units and given jobs that required lesser skills. All armed forces, male and female, were racially segregated until the Korean War.

Women aviators partially broke through this sex-role stereotyping. In 1939 two well-known women pilots, Jacqueline Cochran and Nancy Harkness Love, tried unsuccessfully to convince Army Air Force officials to use women to fly noncombat missions. But in 1942 the British Air Transport Authority asked Cochran to organize American women pilots to ferry planes to England. The program was successful. By 1943 the increased airplane production in the United States required more pilots than could be found among men. The Women Airforce Service Pilots (WASP) was established to close the gap.

Logging over sixty million miles, the WASP ferried planes throughout the United States and Canada. They flew transport planes, B-29 bombers, and fighter craft. They towed targets while gunner trainees fired live bullets at the targets. They flew simulated strafing tests—attacking ground troops with machine-gun fire from low-flying aircraft—and radar-jamming and searchlight-tracking missions.

In an oral interview Jacqueline Cochran, who headed the WASP, speaks about the women pilots' bravery and skill testing planes considered so dangerous that men pilots refused to test them.

Q: During the Second World War you did a great deal to get women pilots used properly, to get them recognized?

Cochran: Actually, I got called to General Arnold's office late in 1940 and found Air Marshal Harris, Chief of the British Mission, there. Arnold said they needed pilots desperately for ferrying airplanes to England and other places and asked me if I could be of any help. I said I would be happy to volunteer and fly some of them over for them if they wanted me to and my services were immediately accepted.

I got to Canada and found there a large group of American men. Many of them were fine pilots but many of them were what I call riff-raff, getting enormous amounts of money tax free for this particular job. Some of them threatened to quit if they let "that woman fly" but I said: "Let them bluff—they won't quit." And of course they didn't. It was a difficult task, dangerous and with a high mortality rate. Planes and pilots just disappeared en route. You never heard of them again.

Q: You got shot at on the trip?

Cochran: Yes, I got shot at over the North Atlantic. Others did too. You couldn't see out. It was overcast and you couldn't tell whether the shots came from our forces or from the enemy. Apparently they were just trigger happy.

In England, they asked me if I could recruit a group of American women. If they could fly as well as they thought I could, they wanted them. I came back then and recruited forty women. Fifteen of the forty were turned down in Canada for lack of efficiency. All twenty-five filled their contracts and some stayed until the war was over. Only one of the twenty-five girls was killed. They were all used in ferrying work. I ferried for eleven months.

We landed planes like the Hurricane and the Spitfire in fields where today I wouldn't put my Lodestar if I could avoid it. When planes were damaged in combat the boys often put them down on the first field. We would then take the damaged aircraft and fly to a depot. Again—when a mission was being organized, Ferry Pilots would assemble the planes. We would fly perhaps five different types in a single day, to a certain field. After the planes were returned to the field, when the mission was over, we would disperse them and put them on satellite fields—two or three planes to a field.

In September 1942 Cochran convinced General Arnold that she be allowed to train women pilots as part of the U.S. Army Air Force.

Cochran: We started out our first training program. The girls proved to be simply remarkable. There were only two disciplinary cases out of two thousand girls. When the time came and they were ready to be part of the Air Force, I went to see General Arnold and said: "The girls are ready to do you proud and the country proud as a part of your Air Force. I have only one complaint, however—the attrition is rather high through marriage; seems that maybe it is part of the wartime hysteria of people getting married."

I got a call one day to come into General Arnold's office. I was down in Fort Worth. I stayed down there for

about nine months in the early period to be close to the
Training Command program. So I came up from Texas
to see him.

He said, "What do you know about the B-26?"

I said, "I don't know a thing except scuttlebut—that it
won't substitute for an airplane. The wings are too small,
etc."

Arnold said, "I want you to go out and fly it and tell
me what you think about it."

I said, "I can cure your men of walking off the program."
They were, you know, and they were saying that they couldn't
fly the plane. They were willing to be killed in a war but
they wouldn't fly this plane.

Arnold asked me how and I said, "Just put some girl
pilots on."

Arnold said, "But what if you kill some of them?"

And I said, "Suppose I do—there is no difference if
a woman is killed or a man if the program has to go forward—and this one has to go forward!"

Anyway, I went out and flew the plane and didn't see
anything so difficult about it. I knew if you lost an engine
on the takeoff, chances were you weren't going to get away
with it. Then it was like flying a single engine plane and
you had to accept the fact that it was not two motored. If
you had a pretty short field to get into, it was pretty hard
to do it—you had to accept that it had a high landing
speed and keep to a field that could accommodate it.

I went out and flew [the B-26] and came back and said
that there was nothing wrong with it. "They are a bunch
of sissies. I am really mad about it. Let's put on the girls."

We subsequently had 150 girls flying the B-26. I mean the A model—the difficult ones for the most part, because they did finally enlarge the wing area to give better landing characteristics. The girls were towing targets while live bullets were being shot at the targets from B-24s. They did seventy thousand operational hours of this tow work [and] there was only one minor accident and not a single fatality.

They also did radio control work which was under [security "wraps"]. One girl would fly the airplane and another girl would sit beside her and, by remote control, fly another without anybody in it. She would control the other airplane over the target line where men on the ground with A/C guns would shoot the plane down. It was an exceedingly difficult operation and hazardous, but we never had a fatality on that. We did have seven girls killed by sabotage.

The girls ferried, of course, but did no overseas work at all. I was the only woman to ferry any airplane of any nationality over the ocean during the war . . . another first!

Despite the important work of the WASP, Congress voted against changing their status from that of a civilian unit. When the war ended, the women pilots were not eligible for any military and veteran benefits, or military honors. The surviving families of those who had been killed in the line of duty received none of the benefits other survivors received, either. In 1977 Congress finally voted the WASP veteran status.

You Should Be Home with the Children

When the war ended in 1945, women found themselves back in the kitchen. As war production plants
closed, women workers were laid off. Returning veter-
ans, having risked their lives for their country, felt
entitled to their old jobs, and trade unions agreed
that they should have them. Women were fired or
demoted to poorer-paying jobs that required lesser
skills. With opportunities closing in heavy industry
and manufacturing, women moved back into lower-
paying traditional women's jobs—office work, nursing,
teaching, and social work.

The message to "stay home" was proclaimed in
postwar government information, popular books, and
mass-circulation women's magazines. Women were
again urged to devote their lives to the sacred institutions of home, family, and motherhood. Dr. Benjamin
Spock's *Common Sense Book of Baby and Child Care*
became the Bible of baby care for millions of Americans. Dr. Spock's book told parents to be loving instead
of punitive, and not to be overprotective—important
advances in the commonly held attitudes about child
care. However, it unwittingly contributed to the movement to make women feel guilty for their natural desires
to accomplish more in their lives than raising chil-

dren—important as that is. Spock told women that though he accepted that there were some mothers who had to work outside the home for economic reasons, a child needed a steady loving person in life. The mother was the best one to provide a child with a feeling of belonging and safety. He urged mothers to stay at home until children went to the first grade, unless a good nursery school could be found.

Psychiatrists, reviving the notion of the "woman's sphere" from the nineteenth century, stated that motherhood and wifehood were the natural fulfillment of women's biological functions. Having a career, they said, required aggressiveness, drive, and a taste for competition—unnatural characteristics for women, whose natures were passive, protective, and nurturing. They insisted that pursuing a career harmed women by throwing them into conflict as they tried to balance the demands of the job against the demands of the home.

Women's magazines also praised the virtues of domestic life for women. Advertisements showed happy women serving their husbands nutritious casseroles, diapering their babies, and washing their infants' and husband's clothes. Magazine articles confirmed that raising babies, running a home, and being sweet and submissive to one's husband was a woman's most impor-

A NEW AND WONDERFUL

General Electric *Roto-Cold* Refrigerator that keeps food so very fresh...so safe...so tasty!

New G-E *Roto-Cold*

Cold air rotates like this, assures safe food protection throughout.

Right from the top to the very bottom of the new G-E Roto-Cold Refrigerator, cold air flows uniformly. (Your own thermometer will prove that there is practically no variation in degrees.)

All foods—no matter where they're placed—are fully refrigerated, fully protected.

In your present refrigerator—like millions in use today —temperatures may vary as much as 16 degrees from top to bottom shelf.

Imagine the effect such changing, warmer temperatures have on the flavors, vitamins and nutritive values of the foods you eat day after day.

With new General Electric Roto-Cold, all foods are *fully* refrigerated, *fully* protected.

See the new G-E Refrigerator with Roto-Cold today. It is priced LOW—costs no more than models without this feature. Look for the name of your nearest G-E dealer in the classified telephone book. General Electric Co., Louisville 2, Ky.

ABOUT
$3.90*
A WEEK

*After down payment. See your dealer for details.
Other G-E Refrigerators priced as low as $219.95.

Advertisement from 1950

tant work. Here is an excerpt from a typical article printed in 1951 in a mass-circulation women's magazine that encouraged women to stay at home.

JUST OVER A year ago, I was suffering from that feeling of guilt and despondency familiar to most working mothers who have small children. During the hours I spent in the office, an accusing voice charged continuously, "You should be home with the children." I couldn't have agreed more, which only created an additional tension: the frustrated anger of one who knows what is right but sees no way of doing it.

A year has passed, and I've had time to judge the advantages and disadvantages of leaving my office job. Here is my balance sheet of the results to date.

Lost

The great alibi: work. My job, and the demands it made on me, were my always accepted excuses for everything and anything: for spoiled children, neglected husband, mediocre food; for being late, tired, preoccupied, conversationally limited, bored, and boring.

The weekly check. And with that went many extravagances and self-indulgences. I no longer had the pleasure of giving showy gifts (the huge doll, the monogrammed pajamas) and the luxury of saying "My treat."

One baseless vanity. I realize now (and still blush over it) that during my working days I felt that my ability to earn was an additional flower in my wreath of accomplishments. Unconsciously—and sometimes consciously—I thought how nice it was for my husband to have a wife who could *also* bring in money. But one day I realized that my office job was only a substitution for the real job I'd been "hired" for: that of being purely a wife and mother.

The sense of personal achievement. A working woman is someone in her own right, doing work that disinterested parties consider valuable enough to pay for. The satisfactions of housekeeping are many, but they are not quite the same.

Praise for a good piece of work. No one can expect her husband to tell her how beautifully clean she keeps the house or how well she makes the beds.

Found

A role. At first I found it hard to believe that being a woman is something in itself. Though I still wince a little at the phrase "wife and mother," I feel quite sure that these words soon will sound as satisfying to me as "actress" or "buyer" or "secretary" or "president."

Normalcy. My relationship with my children is sounder. I realized that when I worked and we had so little time together, we had all played our "Sunday best." Now I'm myself. I scold, I snap, I listen when I have time. I laugh, I praise, I read to them when I have time. In fact, I'm giving a pretty good representation of a human being, and as the children are going to spend most of their lives trying to get along with human beings, they might as well learn right now that people's behavior is variable.

The luxury of free time. This is one of the crown jewels of retirement. The morning or afternoon that occasionally stretches before me, happily blank, to be filled with a visit to a museum or a movie, a chat with a friend, an unscheduled visit to the zoo with the children, the production of the elaborate dish I'd always meant to try, or simply doing nothing, is a great boon.

Handwork. This may seem trivial but making things at home is one of the pleasures the businesswoman is usually deprived of. Homemade cookies, presents, dresses, parties, and relationships can be worth their weight in gold.

Intimacy. The discovery of unusual and unexpected facets in the imaginations of children, which rarely reveal themselves in brief, tense sessions, is very rewarding.

Improved Appearance. Shinier hair, nicer hands, better manicures, are the products of those chance twenty-minute free periods that turn up in the busiest days of women who don't go to business.

PART EIGHT

THE NEW CONSCIOUSNESS

The Problem That Has No Name

In 1955 Betty Friedan, a 34-year-old suburban house-wife, mother of three small children, and part-time journalist, lived a financially comfortable life in the suburbs. But despite her comforts, Friedan was dissatis-fied with her life and began examining it to figure out why. She sent questionnaires to the women who had graduated with her from Smith College in 1942 to see how they felt about their lives. She interviewed other women like herself. Friedan concluded that these women were confused and unfulfilled but were ashamed to voice their dissatisfactions. Society's message, rein-forced in women's magazines, on television, and by psychologists and other family experts, clearly stated

A family barbecue

that such dissatisfactions were unnatural. Being feminine, being beautiful, finding a husband, bearing children, being a homemaker, was a woman's highest
fulfillment. In her book published in 1963, Friedan
attacked this feminine mystique, and millions of American women listened.

THE SUBURBAN HOUSEWIFE—she was the dream image of
the young American women and the envy, it was said, of
women all over the world. The American housewife—freed

by science and labor-saving appliances from the drudgery, the dangers of childbirth and the illnesses of her grandmother. She was healthy, beautiful, educated, concerned only about her husband, her children, her home. She had found true feminine fulfillment. As a housewife and mother, she was respected as a full and equal partner to man in his world. She was free to choose automobiles, clothes, appliances, supermarkets; she had everything that women ever dreamed of.

In the fifteen years after World War II, this mystique of feminine fulfillment became the cherished and self-perpetuating core of contemporary American culture. Millions of women lived their lives in the image of those pretty pictures of the American suburban housewife, kissing their husbands goodbye in front of the picture window, depositing their stationwagonsful of children at school, and smiling as they ran the new electric waxer over the spotless kitchen. They baked their own bread, sewed their own and their children's clothes, kept their new washing machines and dryers running all day. They changed the sheets on the beds twice a week instead of once, took the rug-hooking class in adult education, and pitied their poor frustrated mothers, who had dreamed of having a career. Their only dream was to be perfect wives and mothers; their highest ambition to have five children and a beautiful house, their only fight to get and keep their husbands. They had no thought for the unfeminine problems of the world outside the home; they wanted the men to make the major decisions. They gloried in their role as women, and wrote proudly on the census blank: "Occupation: housewife."

If a woman had a problem in the 1950's and 1960's, she knew that something must be wrong with her marriage, or with herself. Other women were satisfied with their lives, she thought. What kind of a woman was she if she did not feel this mysterious fulfillment waxing the kitchen floor? She was so ashamed to admit her dissatisfaction that she never knew how many other women shared it. If she tried to tell her husband, he didn't understand what she was talking about. She did not really understand it herself. "There's nothing wrong really," [the women] kept telling themselves. "There isn't any problem."

But on an April morning in 1959, I heard a mother of four, having coffee with four other mothers in a suburban development fifteen miles from New York, say in a tone of quiet desperation, "the problem." And the others knew, without words, that she was not talking about a problem with her husband, or her children, or her home. Suddenly they realized they all shared the same problem, the problem that has no name. They began, hesitantly, to talk about it. Later, after they had picked up their children at nursery school and taken them home to nap, two of the women cried, in sheer relief, just to know that they were not alone.

Gradually I came to realize that the problem that has no name was shared by countless women in America.

If I am right, the problem that has no name stirring in the minds of so many American women today is not a matter of loss of femininity or too much education, or the demands of domesticity. It is far more important than anyone recognizes. It is the key to those other new and old problems which have been torturing women and their husbands and children, and their doctors and educators for years. It may well be the key to our future as a nation and a culture.

We can no longer ignore that voice within women that says: "I want something more than my husband and my children and my home."

The feminine mystique says that the highest value and the only commitment for women is the fulfillment of their own femininity. It says that the great mistake of Western culture, through most of its history, has been the undervaluation of this femininity. It says this femininity is so mysterious and intuitive and close to the creation and origin of life that man-made science may never be able to understand it. But however special and different, it is in no way inferior to the nature of man; it may even in certain respects be superior. The mistake, says the mystique, the root of women's troubles in the past is that women envied men, women tried to be like men, instead of accepting their own nature, which can find fulfillment only in sexual passivity, male domination, and nurturing maternal love.

The new mystique makes the housewife-mothers, who never had a chance to be anything else, the model for all women; it presupposes that history has reached a final and glorious end in the here and now, as far as women are concerned.

The core of the problem for women today is not sexual but a problem of identity—a stunting or evasion of growth that is perpetuated by the feminine mystique. It is my thesis that as the Victorian culture did not permit women to accept or gratify their basic sexual needs, our culture does not permit women to accept or gratify their basic need to grow and fulfill their potentialities as human beings, a need which is not solely defined by their sexual role.

There have been identity crises for man at all crucial turning points in human history. For the first time in their history, women are becoming aware of an identity crisis in their own lives, a crisis which began many generations ago, and will not end until they, or their daughters, turn an unknown corner and make of themselves and their lives the new image that so many women now so desperately need.

She Is Not Free Until I Am Free

The financially comfortable life of white middle-class women after World War II was not shared by most black women. Racism, even violence against them, as well as the indignity of segregation, did not cease despite legal and political efforts by black organizations and individuals. On May 17, 1954, in the case *Brown vs. Topeka Board of Education*, the Supreme Court over-turned the *Plessy vs. Ferguson* decision (the legitimization of the "separate but equal" concept) and declared that school segregation was unconstitutional. This momentous decision set the stage for the modern civil rights movement.

In 1955 six black girls and three black boys were enrolled in the all-white Little Rock High School. They encountered so much violence by white segregationists that President Dwight D. Eisenhower called in the National Guard to protect them. That same year Rosa Parks, a seamstress and longtime civil-rights activist in Montgomery, Alabama, refused to move to the back of a segregated bus and was arrested. For the next year Montgomery's blacks walked to work instead of riding the buses to protest segregation in public transportation and other facilities. The success of the boycott in ending segregation in Montgomery spurred confidence that similar nonviolent protests could force other southern cities to change their policies.

For the next ten years similar mass protests sprang up across the nation as black Americans, supported by many whites, challenged racial discrimination in all walks of life. Black high school and college students were beaten and arrested; fire hoses were turned on them when they had sit-ins at segregated restaurants and bus stations. A confederation of civil-rights organizations launched massive voter-registration drives to overcome the obstacles used by white racists to deprive blacks of their right to vote. But racists continued to use violence to try to intimidate the civil-rights activists.

In 1962 Fannie Lou Hamer, a sharecropper in Ruleville, Mississippi, went to the courthouse to register to vote. Soon afterward she was fired from her job, her house was bombed, and she was thrown off the land she had sharecropped for years.

Mrs. Hamer was not intimidated. She became a field secretary for the Student Nonviolent Coordinating Committee, SNCC, and helped others to register. In 1964 she ran for Congress on the Mississippi Freedom Party ticket. In this speech given before an integrated audience, Hamer talks about the superiority that shaped and distorted white women's feelings toward black women. In stating that white women will never have true liberation until their black sisters are free, she echoes the words of Sojurner Truth and the Grimké sisters 120 years ago.

THE SPECIAL PLIGHT and role of black women is not something that just happened three years ago. We've had a special plight for 350 years. My grandmother had it. My grandmother was a slave.

It's been a special plight for the black woman. But you know, sometimes I really feel more sorrier for the white woman than I feel for ourselves because she has been caught up in this thing, caught up feeling very special, and folks, I'm going to put it on the line, because my job is not to make people feel comfortable. You've been caught up in this thing because, you know, you worked my grandmother, and after that you worked my mother, and then finally you got hold of me. And you really thought, people—you might try to cool it now, but I been watching you, baby. You thought you was *more* because you was a woman, and especially a white woman, you had this kind of angel feeling that you were untouchable. You know that? There's nothing under the sun that made you believe that you was just like me, that under this white pigment of skin is red blood, just like under this black skin of mine. So we was used as black women over and over and over. You know, I remember a time when I was working around white people's house, and one thing that would make me mad as hell, after I would be done slaved all day long, this white woman would get on the phone, calling some of her friends, and said, "You know, I'm tired, because *we* have been working," and I said, "That's a damn lie." You're not used to that language, honey, but I'm gone tell you where it's *at*. So all of these things was happened because you *had* more. You had been put on a pedestal, and then not only put on a pedestal, but you had been put in something like an ivory castle. So what happened to you, we have busted the castle open and whacking like hell for the pedestal. And when you hit the ground, you're gone have to fight like hell, like we've been fighting all this time.

In the past, I don't care how poor this white woman was, in the South she still felt like she was more than us. In the North, I don't care how poor or how rich this white woman has been, she still felt like she was more than us. But coming to the realization of the thing, her freedom is shackled in chains to mine, and she realizes for the first time that she is not free until I am free.

The mass protests and courage of black Americans spurred a new era of reform in which women participated as much as men. Indians, Mexican Americans, Puerto Ricans, and other minorities demanded equality and compensation for past injustices. White college students supported minority protests, and began their own movement against the American military presence in Vietnam. Women Strike for Peace, an organization of housewives and mothers, marched and lobbied for a nuclear weapons test ban treaty. Women were important participants in all these movements.

It's in Your Own Head

Dolores Huerta traces her family's roots back to 1600 in New Mexico. Her father was a migrant worker who followed the harvest through the west. When her parents divorced, her mother settled her and her brother near Stockton, California, where she opened a small café. To earn extra money for the family, Huerta's brother picked tomatoes in the field and she packed them in the plant. She was keenly aware through high school and college that she was discriminated against because she was a Chicana, the name given to Mexican immigrants and U.S. citizens of Mexican ancestry.

In the 1960s Chicano farm workers formed a union, the United Farm Workers (UFW), to better their economic situation. Huerta quickly joined up as a union organizer. At that time farm workers, who hand-picked grapes and lettuce, lived in desperate poverty. They earned about $1.40 an hour. They had no unemployment insurance for the time between harvests. They had no health insurance to pay bills when they got sick.

Cesar Chavez, the driving organizer and spiritual force of the farm workers, encouraged women to take leading roles as union organizers. For Chicanas, brought up in a society where husbands ruled and women obeyed, such activism threatened not only the men but the women's own sense of their appropriate roles in life. In this interview in 1974, Huerta speaks of how she felt at first about her dual role as mother and organizer, and about the roles of other Chicanas in the union.

I HAD A lot of doubts to begin with, but I had to act in spite of my conflict between my family and my commitment. My biggest problem was not to feel guilty about it. I don't any more, but then, everybody used to lay these guilt trips on me, about what a bad mother I was, neglecting my children. My own relatives were the hardest, especially when my kids were small—I had six and one on the way when I started—and I was driving around Stockton with all these little babies in the car, the different diapers for each one.

It's always hard, not just because you're a woman but because it's hard to really make that commitment. It's in your own head. I'm sure my own life was better because of my involvement. I was able to go through a lot of very serious personal problems and survive them because I had something else to think about. Otherwise, I might have gotten engulfed in my personal difficulties and, I think, I probably would have gone under.

The way I first got away from feeling guilty about neglecting my family was a religious cop-out, I guess. I had serious doubts whether I was doing the right thing, giving kids a lousy supper to go to a council meeting. So I would pray and say, if what I was doing wasn't bearing fruit, then it would be a sign I shouldn't be doing it. When good things came out of my work, when it bore fruit, I took that as a sign I should continue and that the sacrifices my family and I were making were justified.

We haven't had a stable place to live—I haven't been anywhere for more than two months—since 1970. But taking my kids all over the states made them lose their fears of people, of new situations. Most of us have to be mobile.

There is an undercurrent of discrimination against women in our own organization, even though Cesar goes out of his way to see that women have leadership positions. Cesar always felt strongly about women in the movement. This time, no married man went out on the boycott unless he took his wife. We find day care in the cities so the women can be put on the picket line with the men. It's a great chance for participation. Of course we take it for granted now that women will *want* to be as involved as men. But in the beginning, at the first meetings, there were only men. And a certain discrimination still exists. Cesar—and other men—treat us differently. Cesar's stricter with the women, he demands more of us. But the more I think of it, the more I'm convinced that the women have gotten stronger because he expects so much of us. You could even say it's gotten lopsided—women are stronger than the men.

Women in the union are great on the picket line. More staying power, and we're nonviolent. One of the reasons our union *is* nonviolent is that we want our women and children involved, and we stay nonviolent because of the women and children. Excluding women, protecting them, keeping women at home, that's the middle-class way. Poor people's movements have always had whole families on the line, ready to move at a moment's notice, with more courage because that's all we had. It's a class not an ethnic thing.

What Got You Interested in the Women's Movement?

In 1961, as the civil-rights movement was waging its battle against racism, Esther Peterson, head of the Women's Bureau and Assistant Secretary of Labor, urged President John F. Kennedy to set up a Presidential Commission on the Status of Women, with Eleanor Roosevelt as the head. Peterson wanted to encourage more women to join the work force and to promote laws guaranteeing women equal pay for equal work.

She also wanted to settle the question of the Equal Rights Amendment (ERA), whose passage she felt would adversely affect protective labor laws for which women's groups had fought so hard.

The Commission's investigation confirmed that women, like other minority groups, were victims of discrimination and injustice. Among the Commission's many recommendations were the setting up of education facilities for adults and child-care services for families, and the revision of sex-discriminatory Social Security benefits and unemployment insurance. To promote equal work opportunities, the Commission recommended paid maternity leaves and the promotion of women to upper-level government jobs. The Commission rejected the ERA, insisting that if the Fifth and Fourteenth amendments of the Constitution, which guarantee all citizens equal protection under the laws, were enforced, then there was no need for it.

In the next three years Congress passed three laws that helped women fight sex discrimination in the courts. The first law was the 1963 Equal Pay Act. Although this law excluded farm and domestic workers, it confirmed the widespread practice of unequal pay for equal work between men and women. Title VII of the 1964 Civil Rights Law forbade both racial and sexual discrimination in employment. Executive Order

11246 (amended in 1967) forbade discrimination in hiring because of race, color, religion, sex, or national origin in all federally contracted work.

Some women found these laws and other government actions insufficient to make the necessary changes that would equalize treatment of women and men in society. In 1966 thirty women, including Betty Friedan, founded the National Organization for Women (NOW) "to take action to bring American women into full participation in the mainstream of American society."

By 1970 many other women's groups had been formed. Feminism—the idea that women were entitled to political, social, and economic equality with men— was heard and felt in cities and towns across the United States. Women brought lawsuits to challenge discrimination in the workplace, schools, and courts. Women lobbied for government-supported day-care centers, passage of the Equal Rights Amendment, and new state and federal laws against sexual discrimination. They organized educational campaigns to inform women of their rights. They marched in the streets to dramatize their right to control their reproductive lives by the repeal of antiabortion laws. Lesbian women, along with homosexual men, asserted the need for gay rights, their demand that society abolish discrimination against them for their different sexual lifestyle.

Women's Equality Day, August 26, 1977

A group of younger women—activists of the civil rights, student, and antiwar movements—began to question what had happened to them in these movements. They had picketed side by side with men, and been arrested, beaten, and jailed, but few had been leaders and decision makers. Like their foremothers in the abolition movement, these activists concluded that their male allies did not include women in their ideas about equality. This male superiority damaged women as much as white superiority damaged people of color. The women tried to explore this concept with their male comrades, but were mostly rebuffed.

Some women activists began meeting weekly in small discussion groups without leaders. Six to twelve women sat in a circle and each spoke in turn on an agreed-upon topic concerning her life. They talked about their families, childhood, school, sex, marriage, and motherhood. After everyone talked, the women explained what they had learned listening to each other. They saw how similar their lives and problems were. They concluded that their problems stemmed from being female in a male-dominated society. They found that sexism oppressed women and kept them from developing their full powers. They realized that women were still defined as having a separate sphere and were trained from infancy to be feminine, passive, nurturing, and noncompetitive. Women who refused to submit to such roles were mocked, squelched, and attacked as unfeminine and abnormal. The term "consciousness raising" was coined to describe this process by which women educated themselves to understand that personal experiences were connected to political, social, and economic conditions.

After a few months of talking, many groups moved on to direct action, to try to change something that they considered a problem. They organized child-care centers for mothers who wanted more free time or to resume careers. They set up rape crisis centers to help women recuperate from the trauma of sexual violence. The media informed thousands of other women about these consciousness-raising groups. Soon women who had never been involved in political groups formed their own consciousness-raising groups. Red-stockings and the Radical Feminists, two New York City groups, put together questions to help new groups get started. Here are some of those questions.

WEEK 1 GENERAL: What are some of the things that got you interested in the women's movement? Why did you want to join this group? What do you think the group will be like? Tell about your background and how you came to be at this meeting.

WEEK 2 FAMILY: How did each of your parents relate to you as a girl (daughter)? Were you treated differently from brothers or boyfriends? What did you do as a little girl that was different from what little boys did? Did you ever want to do anything else?

WEEK 3 FAMILY: Discuss your relationships with women in your family.

WEEK 4 CHILDHOOD AND ADOLESCENCE: What were your problems growing up as a girl? How did you learn what "feminine" meant? Did you have heroines or heros? Who were they? What were your favorite games? How did you feel about your body changing at puberty? How did you feel when you had your first period?

WEEK 5 MEN: Discuss your relationships with men—friends, lovers, bosses—as they evolved. Are there any recurring patterns?

WEEK 6 MARITAL STATUS: How do (or did) you feel about being single? Married? Divorced? What have been the pressures—family, social—on you? Why did you marry the man you did?

WEEK 7 MOTHERHOOD: Did you consider having children a matter of choice? What social or personal pressures made you feel you should become a mother? Do you enjoy taking care of your children? What hopes do you have for your daughter? For your son? Why are these hopes different? What have been your experiences and thoughts about child care, contraception and abortion?

WEEK 8 SEX: What was your first sexual experience? How do you feel about petting? What is a "nice girl"? Were you a "nice girl"? Have you ever felt that men pressured you into having sexual relations? Have you ever lied about having an orgasm?

WEEK 9 SEX: When do you feel like a sex object? How do you feel about your body? your face? Do you want to be beautiful? Do you ever feel invisible?

WEEK 10 WOMEN: What are your relationships with other women? Have you ever felt competitive with other women for men? Have you ever felt attracted to another woman?

WEEK 11 BEHAVIOR: What is a "nice girl"? Have you ever been called selfish? What have you done to please others even when it's displeased you? Why?

WEEK 12 AGING: How do you feel about getting old? About your mother getting old? What parts of aging do you look forward to? What parts do you fear? How is aging different for men and women?

WEEK 13 AMBITIONS: What would you most like to do in life? What has kept you from doing it?

WEEK 14 MOVEMENT ACTIVITY: What are some of the things you would like to see the women's movement accomplish?

Why I Want a Wife

Discrimination against women—or, in a more general sense, the attitudes that promoted the stereotyping of women's roles—came to be known as "sexism." Feminist critiques of sexism in American life appeared in mimeographed booklets, popular magazines, best-selling books, and on television talk shows. The feminists showed how sexism was entrenched in all institutions—school, church, government, relationships between men and women, and family.

Feminist educators documented how history texts ignored women's contributions. They showed how school readers stereotyped boys as active (Dick runs), girls as passive (Jane watches him run), women as homemakers (Mother bakes), men as wage earners (Father works). Feminists attacked prominent psychologists such as Sigmund Freud and Helen Deutsch for defining women as innately passive. They showed how TV and magazine advertising portrayed women's lives as revolving around the kitchen, the laundry room, and the bedroom.

Theologian Mary Daly showed how the Catholic Church oppressed women by refusing to have altar girls or women priests, and by forbidding women to use contraception. Theorist Anne Koedt challenged the long-accepted views about female sexuality; she stated that the center of a woman's orgasm was not the vagina, but a small external organ called the clitoris. Her thesis was confirmed by major sex researchers. Koedt suggested that male-female sexual relationships had to be changed for mutual sexual enjoyment. Other feminists documented the history of rape, wife beating, sexual harassment, and pornography. They pointed out that these acts had almost nothing to do with sexuality but were rather connected with violence, rage, and the need to dominate.

Feminists analyzed how traditional family life oppressed women. Judy Syfers, a member of Sudsofloppen, a California women's group, used humor to take on the serious topic of the division of labor and sex-role stereotyping in the traditional family, in which men provide economic security and women take care of the home, the children, and the husbands.

I BELONG TO that classification of people known as wives. I am A Wife. And, not altogether incidentally, I am a mother.

Not too long ago a male friend of mine appeared on the scene from the Midwest fresh from a recent divorce.

He had one child, who is, of course, with his ex-wife. He is obviously looking for another wife. As I thought about him while I was ironing one evening, it suddenly occurred to me that I, too, would like to have a wife. Why do I want a wife?

I would like to go back to school so that I can become economically independent, support myself, and, if need be, support those dependent upon me. I want a wife who will work and send me to school. And while I am going to school I want a wife to take care of my children. I want a wife to keep track of the children's doctor and dentist appointments. And to keep track of mine, too. I want a wife to make sure my children eat properly and are kept clean. I want a wife who will wash the children's clothes and keep them mended. I want a wife who is a good nurturant attendant to my children, arranges for their schooling, makes sure that they have an adequate social life with their peers, takes them to the park, the zoo, etc. I want a wife who takes care of the children when they are sick, a wife who arranges to be around when the children need special care, because, of course, I cannot miss classes at school. My wife must arrange to lose time at work and not lose the job. It may mean a small cut in my wife's income from time to time, but I guess I can tolerate that. Needless to say, my wife will arrange and pay for the care of the children while my wife is working.

I want a wife who will take care of *my* physical needs. I want a wife who will keep my house clean. A wife who will pick up after my children, a wife who will pick up after me. I want a wife who will keep my clothes clean, ironed, mended, replaced when need be, and who will see to it that my personal things are kept in their proper place so that I can find what I need the minute I need it. I want a wife who cooks the meals, a wife who is a *good* cook. I want a wife who will plan the menus, do the necessary grocery shopping, prepare the meals, serve them pleasantly, and then do the cleaning up while I do my studying. I want a wife who will care for me when I am sick and sympathize with my pain and loss of time from school. I want a wife to go along when our family takes a vacation so that someone can continue to care for me and my children when I need a rest and a change of scene.

I want a wife who will not bother me with rambling complaints about a wife's duties. But I want a wife who will listen to me when I feel the need to explain a rather difficult point I have come across in my course of studies. And I want a wife who will type my papers for me when I have written them.

I want a wife who will take care of the details of my social life. When my wife and I are invited out by my friends, I want a wife who will take care of the babysitting arrangements. When I meet people at school that I like and want to entertain, I want a wife who will have the house clean, will prepare a special meal, serve it to me and my friends, and not interrupt when I talk about the things that interest me and my friends. And I want a wife who knows that sometimes I need a night out by myself.

I want a wife who is sensitive to my sexual needs, a wife who makes love passionately and eagerly when I feel like it, a wife who makes sure that I am satisfied. And, of course, I want a wife who will not demand sexual attention when I am not in the mood for it. I want a wife who assumes the complete responsibility for birth control, because I do not want more children. I want a wife who will remain sexually faithful to me so that I do not have to clutter up my intellectual life with jealousies. And I want a wife who understands that *my* sexual needs may entail more than strict adherence to monogamy. I must, after all, be able to relate to people as fully as possible.

If, by chance, I find another person more suitable as a wife than the wife I already have, I want the liberty to replace my present wife with another. Naturally, I will expect a fresh, new life; my wife will take the children and be solely responsible for them so that I am left free.

When I am through with school and have acquired a job, I want my wife to quit working and remain at home, so that my wife can more fully and completely take care of a wife's duties.

My God, who wouldn't want a wife?

The Gay Movement Helped Me Have a Family

For many lesbians, the gay movement was their first opportunity to protest society's discrimination against their sexual preference. The movement also offered a public platform from which to work together to protect their civil rights. For some gay women, who had grown up in a society that valued only heterosexuality, the movement was the first time they openly realized their sexual preference and could take pride in it. Diane Bratcher was born in 1952 and attended college in the 70s, during the beginning of the women's movement and the modern gay movement. She speaks of the sexual attitudes that she experienced growing up in the midwest, her realization that she was a lesbian, and the effect that the gay movement had on her life.

I GREW UP in the country, about fifteen miles outside Cincinnati, Ohio, where there were sheep and cow farms. When I was six they built Interstate 75 about a quarter of a mile from where we lived, and suddenly farms were sold to the state and divided up. My family was poor. My father was a school-bus driver during the day and at night he worked as a clerk on the railroad. My mother worked at home.

When I was little, I was a tomboy and played mostly with boys. About the time I got my period, when I was about twelve, my mother told me I was getting a little too old to play with the boys. So I began playing with girls. From then on almost all my friends were girls.

The worst thing that could happen to a girl in those days was for her to get pregnant. My mother instilled that in me. She talked about the girl down the street who got pregnant and had to give away her baby and how horrible that was. The signal was clear. It was better to be with girls than with boys.

When I was about twelve, I fell in love with another girl in the Girl Scout troop. I wrote her long love letters and she answered them. I hid the letters and all my feelings in that experience from my parents, like kids hide most things from their parents. I went to Catholic grade school, where I learned to hide everything from the nuns and from all adults. So being in love with this girl was something I would never tell my mother about.

I didn't figure out that this was my sexual preference until I was in college. I was there from 1970 to 1974. It was the end of the Vietnam War. The women's movement was growing, but a large-scale gay movement hadn't really gotten started. I was part of a college consciousness-raising group where we read and discussed books by such women as Robin Morgan and Shulamith Firestone. Firestone put forth the theory that the logical extension of feminism was to be a lesbian, the woman-identified woman. And when we read that, all of a sudden, three or four of the women in the group, including me, figured out what we were. What previously had been hanging out with women, identifying with women, now became obvious. We were lesbians, and it was okay.

That experience was the end of my struggle to try to be straight. It made sense, and it felt good to me and the other women. We had a philosophical rationale for our lesbianism. We had support from the political stand. We realized the reason we hadn't known we were lesbians before was because nobody ever talked about it. There were no role models for us, no people who were publicly gay who we could relate to, no unmarried aunts or uncles who were openly gay. We didn't know of or hear of any identifiable gay lifestyle. At least not in Ohio. Maybe there was in New York.

In terms of my parents' generation, homosexuality was never talked about as a possibility for one's children.

For seven years, I was involved with a woman I met in college. My whole family knew her and liked her very much, but I never discussed directly with my parents that we were lovers. Eventually I did tell my sisters. After college, my roommate and I moved from Ohio to New York. We had two miniature collies that my mother called the grand-dogs. She hung the dogs' pictures on her living room wall like you hang pictures of grandchildren. But we never talked about lesbianism. I think my mother knew. I doubt my father knew.

When I broke up with this woman, my sisters were very supportive and sympathetic. They treated it like a divorce. They told me that my mother was very concerned about me. But she never spoke to me about it, or said let's talk, or come home, like she might have had it been a man I had broken up with.

When my little sister wanted to move to New York, I knew I had to tell her I was gay. I knew I had to do it directly. I said it on the phone, "Sissie, there's only one important thing that I have to make sure you understand. I'm a lesbian and most of my friends are women. So you won't be meeting too many guys through me." She said, "Do you think I'm stupid? I've known for years." She had come to visit me in New York when she was fifteen and she said she knew even then.

I don't think being gay has ever affected my work life. At least not in any direct way that I know of. Maybe if I lived a more traditional lifestyle, I might have tried to hide who I am. But I work for a church organization in a political job that concerns what I think are the most important political issues of our time—opposition to apartheid, promoting peace and equality, ending racism. I grew up in the sixties. It was a very idealistic time when ideas like justice and freedom were very important. I grew up thinking that people had an obligation to do the right thing, to be in public service, and to help change the world.

I've always sought jobs that would make a difference changing the world, and fortunately I've worked with people who were openminded and progressive. So in a sense I've made a choice to work in places that pursue social change.

That doesn't mean that I went into my job and made statements about my sexual preference, but I know that my co-workers are openminded about different kinds of families. Everyone at work knows my partner is a woman. I talk about her at work. Over the twelve years I've worked here, my boss and co-workers have learned a lot about my life. They were supportive when my seven-year relationship broke up, and when my mother died, just like good people are.

The gay movement has helped me have a family, with my woman-lover partner, that's equivalent to the family of heterosexual people. It's equivalent to any family where people aren't legally married in the eyes of the state. The gay movement has allowed me to be public about being different.

It's also changed the attitudes of heterosexuals. More

people accept and respect gay people. Most people accept alternative families. The gay movement made that possible for lesbians and gay men, just like the civil rights movement enabled blacks to aspire to be all that they can be. Just like the women's movement helped break down barriers for women to help them fulfill their potential. I suppose you can hide being a lesbian if you want, but gay people don't want to hide. We want what everyone wants—the freedom to be good citizens; to provide for our families, and to live full lives.

I Just Couldn't Have Another Baby

One of the most controversial issues raised by the women's movement was a woman's right to an abortion. Feminists insisted this private decision to end a pregnancy should be made by the person it most affects, and not by lawmakers or doctors. The right to abortion, like the right to birth control, was part of a woman's self-determination, her right to own and control her body. Many feminists felt abortion had to become a personal liberty, a choice among many choices one made in life.

In the 1960s most states had antiabortion laws that had been in existence since the Comstock Laws of 1873. In some states legal abortion was available when a woman's life was threatened, but the "threat" had

to be proven and approved by a panel of doctors. In
the absence of other options, as many as 200,000,
perhaps even a million, women resorted to illegal abortions each year. Performed usually by inexperienced
nonmedical personnel, usually in order to make money,
these abortions caused many deaths, or did permanent
damage to women's internal organs that made future
childbearing impossible.

In the 1960s feminists held public meetings at which
women described their illegal abortions. They demon-
strated in the streets and lobbied legislators to change
the antiabortion laws. In 1973 the Supreme Court,
in the case of *Roe vs. Wade*, ruled that the Sixth
Amendment gave a woman the right to decide whether
or not to have an abortion.

Abortion remains a controversial issue. By 1989
the Supreme Court narrowed the circumstances under
which public funds could be used for abortions and
ruled that the states could impose some restrictions.
Activists on both sides of the issue continue to fight
for their viewpoints.

Here is testimony from four women, as submitted
in a federal court brief, explaining why they chose to
have abortions and what it meant to them:

I AM 38 years old and have had 2 abortions—1 legal, 1
illegal. My first was when I was 19 years old. It was illegal.

I had to drive from North Jersey to Philadelphia for what I understand now was an ineffective treatment by a doctor who sexually abused me while supposedly giving me injections to induce a miscarriage. After a week of treatments (64 injections a day) he used a scalpel to rupture the opening of my uterus. I miscarried later that day. I was too frightened to go to the doctor and developed peritonitis. I almost died.

My second abortion was legal. When I discovered I was pregnant, I went to my doctor, who, with much concern and sympathy, told me of all alternatives, including adoption. We both decided abortion would be best. The procedure was done in a hospital—it took three hours and I was back to work the next week. There was no trauma, other than the difficulty of making a decision that is always hard to make.

~

Now, I am proud to say, I am 6 months pregnant and very excited. We are both looking forward to a child, confident that we are up to meeting this challenge. Things are so different than 5 years ago—now this child will be a wanted child and will come into a loving family waiting for it with open arms. Now we are both ready to give our lives to this new being—before we would have felt robbed.

~

My job on the assembly line at the plant was going well and I needed that job desperately to support the kids. Also I had started night school to improve my chance to get a better job. I just couldn't have another baby—5 kids were enough for me to support. I didn't like the idea of going thru with it. I felt badly for a day or two after the abortion.

But it was the right thing to do. If I had had the baby I would have had to quit my job and go on welfare. Instead I was able to make ends meet and get the kids through school.

~

As for adoption, I very much respect those women having gone that route. It is truly a selfless act of love. But for myself, I knew if I was to have a baby, I would want to keep it. Envisioning what my life would be, an unskilled, unwed mother, my child would not have two parents but one working parent. That's not the life I wanted to give my child and not what I wanted myself. Now almost ten years after, I am married and a full-time mother of two. When we first heard my son's fetal heartbeat I cried tears of joy. Our children were wanted very much and my fantasy is now my life.

Women Should Be Free to Be Anything They Want to Be

Some feminists, such as members of NOW, wanted to reform American institutions so women would have equal opportunity to participate in all aspects of life. Radical feminists, calling their movement women's liberation, did not believe that true emancipation could develop by reforming the system. They felt that eliminating sexism to free women and society from its stunted, distorted view of the "women's sphere" meant transforming or doing away with myths of male superiority and existing male-dominated institutions. Some radical feminists went so far as to propose that since male-female relations inevitably exploited women, only lesbian relationships offered the possibility for equality.

Many American women supported some of the goals of the women's movement, but many disagreed. Some women insisted that femininity was to be treasured; motherhood and homemaking were proud accomplishments and better than most jobs. Some women objected to abortion on religious grounds, citing the belief that life began at conception and thus abortion was the taking of a human life. Many black women believed that race was the major source of their oppression, not sexual discrimination. Women whose identities were largely defined by their roles as mothers, and homemakers felt belittled and alienated from the radical feminists who saw the family as constraining and called for its abolition. Other women viewed all homosexuality as unnatural and did not want it recognized as a legitimate lifestyle.

U.S. Senator Barbara Mikulski identifies herself as one of twenty million women of "European ethnic Catholic descent." At a conference at which women discussed the women's movement, Mikulski, then a member of the House of Representatives, traced the

U.S. Senator Barbara Mikulski

past and present contributions of her constituency in the struggle for women's equality and explained why many of them felt confused, threatened, and demeaned by aspects of the women's movement. They supported child-care facilities, equal educational and work opportunities for women, and programs for senior citizens. But they felt threatened by lifestyle and role changes in the family, which had been the primary source of strength and love throughout the generations of struggle. Mikulski suggests that women accept their diversity and understand that their womanhood links them together despite their differences.

WHEN WE LOOK at the question of fighting for rights, the women in our community have been involved in this struggle for a long time. We go back to the early Trade Union Movement. [We and our mothers and grandmothers and great-grandmothers were the women of the sweatshops. The women who died in the Triangle Shirtwaist fire.] We were "Rosie the Riveter." [And I can tell you something: when World War II was over, and *McCall's* magazine talked about family togetherness and getting out of the factory, you're damn right my aunts and other relatives wanted to get out.]

We're there now when it comes to reforming the work place. We see it in the working class communities around the country where women have organized. And it is interesting that this struggle is not necessarily for their own benefit, but is carried on in behalf of others, which has so often been the story of women.

One of the things that has always held us together—whether it was the 1,000 years of oppression in Czechoslovakia, in Poland, in Latvia or Estonia—is the concept of family. No matter what king, kaiser or czar marched through your country, somehow or other that family would hold you together. The family is not only a living arrangement. It has always been a symbol of survival. When that traditional family structure is challenged by views that some of our people consider as culturally provocative, we feel threatened.

On the other hand, we want equal pay for equal work. We want the benefits that are coming into our communities. We like being out on the barricades. We like bringing about changes. But when threatening ideas come along, we have a tremendous feeling of ambivalence and hurt.

The women in our community are not hostile to the Women's Movement. But we're confused and we're searching. And we're looking to find ways that we can be together. Maybe one of the ways that we can begin to get together is to take a look at our cultural diversity and to respect the different feelings that we have. Respect the ambivalence, respect the reluctance, the shyness and inhibition to participate in some areas.

We have always been taught that diversity has meant conflict in this country. We've always been taught that if we were different, that meant trouble. Yet, diversity—as you can see right here in this room and as you look at our country—is enrichment. If we begin to understand all of these cultural pulls and tugs, then I think we can begin to move toward sisterhood.

To me, women's liberation means that women should be free to be anything they want to be and that we should unite in a common front to remove all barriers that hamper that freedom. To me, that is what we are all about, and I am very glad we're all here today.

PART NINE

WHAT'S AHEAD?

I Have Many Goals

Today American women make up 45 percent of the work force. For most American women work is a necessity, as many are often the sole supporters of their families. It is predicted that by the year 2000, women will make up half the work force. Women have broken into previously closed occupations: one out of five lawyers and doctors are women, and these rates are increasing rapidly. Almost half the accountants and bus drivers are women. But in many occupations women have only token representation. Fewer than 4 percent of America's pilots, mechanics, construction workers, and firefighters are women. Only 3 percent of women hold top-management jobs in America's largest corporations. Though half the population, women are very underrepresented as political leaders.

In 1989 *The New York Times* polled American women to see how they felt about the changes in their lives brought about by working outside the home. Almost half the women said that women had sacrificed too much for their gains in the workplace. In most marriages, women come home after a day of work and begin their second job—cooking, housecleaning, food shopping, bill paying, and child care. Very few have husbands willing to assume housekeeping duties. Eighty-three percent of the working mothers interviewed said they were torn by having to juggle the demands of their jobs and the demands of family life. Many of these women feel stress, fatigue, and resentment over the lopsided division of labor at home but see no way of resolving the dilemma.

In the following interviews, high school girls express their feelings about being female and share their thoughts about their futures.

Seventeen-year-old Yuk Ming Liu is a junior in high school in New York City.

Q: Was there any time in your life that being a girl hindered you?

Yes, in the eighth grade. There was a patrol squad and the teachers only allowed boys to be on it. If you were a monitor, you either brought out the barricades around the school to protect the kids from cars or you stood by the school door and held it for the younger classes. Some monitors guarded the stairwells to maintain order. It just so happened that they only assigned boys to be monitors every year. Some friends of mine and I thought it wasn't fair and we asked the teachers why we couldn't be monitors. They didn't really have an explanation. They said, "It's always been like that, always been the boys' job." When our eighth grade graduated, they started assigning girls.

Q: What do you want to achieve in your life?

I have many goals. Right now my main goal is to get into a good college, like one of the Ivy League schools. I'm split between the medical profession—becoming a psychiatrist, or doing something with languages. I want to continue studying Chinese. I'm also taking Latin, and might want to go into Classics. I want to marry but that will be after I'm set on a career and I know where I'm going. I'm still thinking about having kids but I'm not one hundred percent sure.

Q: How will your life be similar/different from your mother's and grandmother's lives?

My mother expects me to go to college. She had a chance to go to college when she was in Hong Kong. She was accepted but at that time the belief was that a woman didn't have to get a good education, all she had to do was finish high school and then look for a good husband and she would be fine. My mom has taught me that you should be settled before you get married, that you should make sure that you have some kind of foundation for yourself, and that's through getting a good education.

I'm going to be more liberal than my mom. When I was in grade school, she didn't let me go out anywhere—to friends' birthday parties, or even to the library—unless she was with me. I think she felt she had to protect me. We used to have play days after school when the kids got together to mingle; my mom never let me go to them. Now she's more loose and lets me go out once in a while to see a movie or be with friends. She's less strict with my brothers. My mom and I think differently. My mom grew up in a Chinese background. My background is a mixture of Chinese and American views.

My grandmother was born in China and now lives in Hong Kong. She went to school but I don't think she got past high school. Her life was harder than mine. When she was my age, women in China weren't treated equal to men.

Q: If you plan to marry, how do you see your partnership with a man?

I think we'll both work. On weekends, we'll do things with the children. The first few years I might work part-time and be home with the kids. But after that we'll have babysitters—probably someone we know—during the week when we're both working. I wouldn't mind doing the cooking. I think the cleaning should be done by both of us. The decisions should be made collaboratively though I think that making decisions for the children will probably be my job. The husband's job should be to prevent his family from interfering from how we bring up our children. And the woman's job is to bring up the children the correct way.

Q: What would you like women to achieve?

To get to know themselves. There are many women out there who are capable of doing so many things but they just let it go. They don't work at it. They have dreams but the dreams just float away. If you don't do something about the dream it does float away. I think women stop because they get discouraged. They stop pursuing their goals because the society says that girls shouldn't do this or that and they are easily influenced by this attitude. Some girls are lazy. There are other factors, too. Sometimes you're poor or the neighborhood you're brought up in isn't one that makes it easy for you to develop your skills. So a person has to really work to reach the top, to get out of the place they are in and get beyond.

Q: What do you think is the biggest obstacle for women?

The stereotyping of women. People say that they're too aggressive or they're not fit to do a man's job. Some women get really offended by these attitudes and try to change the person's view but some get discouraged when they hear these comments and their dreams start to fall apart slowly.

Seventeen-year-old Keana Bonds is a junior in high school in McComb, Mississippi.

Q: Was there any time in your life that being a girl hindered you?

Not really. If I wanted to do something I could do it. If I wanted to run track being a girl didn't matter. I'm glad to be a girl.

Q: What do you want to achieve in your life?

I want to go to college and study business management. I'm probably not going to stay and work in McComb. I'll probably go to Jackson where there are better jobs with better pay. I want to be married eventually, sometime in my twenties. I really don't want to rush into marriage when I get out of college. I want time to settle down and get a good job first.

Q: How will your life be similar/different from your mother's and grandmother's lives?

I'll be working hard like my mother did for my family. I'll be working at a job so I can give them things they need. I have my mother's ways. I'm softhearted like she is. I think I'll be stricter with my kids than my mother was with us. I don't want my kids to grow up thinking they have the control. My work will be different from my mother's. My mother works now as a clerk in a clothing store. She worked in a hospital for four years. I don't think I'll live in McComb when I'm married.

I'm like my grandmother, my father's mother. She was always on the positive side whatever the situation. I'm understanding and always there for people like she was.

Q: If you plan to marry, how do you see your partnership with a man?

I expect my husband to clean the house and not wait

on me to do it. I expect him to take his share of the responsibility with the children and the bills and the house. I think I'll probably stay home awhile and then go back to work. If I'm at home my husband doesn't have to be there but when he's there, I want him to help. I'm sure I'll keep everything in order. I think I'd rather do the child care than have my husband do it because I think I'll be better at it. I think women are better at it than men.

Q: What do you think is the biggest obstacle women face in achieving their goals?

Sex discrimination is the biggest obstacle. Women can't get certain jobs like construction work. They can't become electricians. Only because they're women.

Q: What would you like women to achieve?

I want them to get higher-paying jobs. Men make more money than women do and I think it's unfair.

Seventeen-year-old Elda D. Cantu is a junior in high school and lives in Mission, Texas.

Q: Was there any time in your life that being a girl hindered you?

No, because when I was small I never saw being a girl as being different. I saw everyone as equals. We played the same games as boys did. My parents never discouraged me in doing anything. They told me, if you want to do it, you try to do your best.

Q: What do you want to achieve in your life?

I want to graduate from high school, go to the University of Texas in Austin, major in education, and teach first or second graders back here in the valley. I plan on getting married after I have a career and am financially set. I also plan on having a family.

Q: How will your life be similar/different from your mother's and grandmother's lives?

Both my mom and grandmother were teachers so in that sense my life will be similar. I'm going to use the values they've taught me for the rest of my life and in my career. They've taught me to achieve what you want. You can't be intimidated by anything. Down here in the valley the majority of people are Hispanic, and if I decide to venture off, maybe to New York, I can't be intimidated by being a minority. They've taught me to be proud of what I am.

I'm kind of old-fashioned. This generation may be materialistic but I'm not going to be trapped in that kind of world.

My grandmother was probably intimidated when she was my age because back then Hispanics weren't highly regarded. She was always thought of as a second-class citizen, though in her heart and within her family, she knew she wasn't.

Q: If you plan to marry, how do you see your partnership with a man?

Right now, I'm kind of scared about marriage because I see so many of my parents' friends getting divorced and separated. If I do marry, I want a fifty-fifty relationship. I want to share finances, housework, responsibilities, problems, and child care.

Q: What do you think is the biggest obstacle women face in achieving their goals?

Intimidation by men is the biggest obstacle. Women are always being stereotyped as being second, behind men. If a woman is applying for the same job as a man, I think she might feel intimidated inside herself because she's scared of just not being able to compete with a man. Being a woman is a bigger obstacle for me than being Hispanic. Of course I'm proud to be a woman, but I'm more proud to be Hispanic. I won't let anyone put me down because I'm Hispanic.

Q: What would you like women to achieve?

I'd like to see a woman president. Women are just as capable as men. I think we came a great deal closer to that goal when Geraldine Ferraro ran for vice-president.

Sixteen-year-old Daisy Rosenblum is a junior in high school in New York City.

Q: Was there any time in your life that being a girl hindered you?

No. And I think there's a reason. Since my parents were both raised in a time when a lot of traditional ideas about how women should lead their lives were being shattered, they raised me to want my own life and make my own decisions. I'm not sure that they consciously decided they were going to instill a new set of values in me, different from the ones they grew up with, but they did. Since I was ten or so I've been making a lot of big decisions for myself. I don't expect to be treated differently or discriminated against. If it's happened already, I haven't seen it.

Q: What would you like to achieve in your life?

I'd like to be an environmental journalist and I'd like to have a family, too. I don't think I can do both at the same time, because this occupation involves a lot of traveling. And aside from traveling, since I love environmental studies and writing, I would probably be immersed in my job, and when I have a family I would really like to give it my full attention. I don't think this has anything to do with being a woman. If whoever I marry decided that he would like to stay home and spend time with our children, then I'd be perfectly willing to go back to work to support the family. I could probably do both things but I want to give each my full involvement. From a practical angle, I may not be able to stop working because we may need the income but I'd certainly slow down when I have a family.

Q: How will your life be similar/different from your mother's and grandmother's?

My mother went to an all-girls' high school and grew up in a different time. This school had a greater impact on her than her era. She was never discriminated against at high school because it was all girls. So when women started becoming feminists, she didn't feel like she needed to assert herself in that way. She asserted herself by doing good work as a person, not a woman. She never expected anyone to treat her differently because she was a woman and neither do I.

My grandmother, my mother's mother, came over from Germany when she was in her teens. My grandfather came from Spain. They both had a lot of Old World values. I think that my grandmother would have liked to work but my grandfather didn't want her to because it would have hurt his pride. And I think that the difference between her life and what my life is and will be is huge. I can't ever imagine meeting a man who would think that way.

Q: If you plan to marry, how do you see your partnership with a man?

I think I already answered that question when I talked about my goals for my life.

Q: What do you think is the biggest obstacle women face in achieving their goals?

There are a lot of girls growing up in homes where their mothers both work and take care of all the housekeeping. I think this demonstrates that we still have a big hump to get over, in terms of men and women dividing up work equally. I think this is a really common situation because a lot of families now need both parents to work, but there's no definition of who's supposed to take care of the kids and all the other household duties. People are still falling back on tradition instead of making new definitions that equalize responsibilities at home between men and women.

Q: What would you like women to achieve?

I wish that women didn't feel that they had to be feminists. I wish women didn't have to know that discrimination exists. I think that if a woman is taught not to expect discrimination and is instilled with the sense that she can do anything she wants to do and that no one can stop her, then she can do it. That's not to say that discrimination isn't a real problem because it is. But I think women can overcome that problem by consistently showing that what they can do is no better or worse than what men can do.

Sixteen-year-old Angel Stimers is a junior in high school and lives in Claverack, New York.

Q: Was there any time in your life that being a girl hindered you?

Kind of. One time I wanted to play basketball in the high school school yard and there were a bunch of guys playing. I wanted to go over and play but I felt like I would feel out of place and I wouldn't fit in, so I didn't go over.

Q: What would you like to achieve in your life?

I enjoy working with computers, specifically programming and organizing bank accounts. I plan to go to college and major in accounting and then get a job up here. I also want to get married and have a small family, one or two kids. I always thought I'd get married when I was about twenty-four. I want to travel all over the world, probably with my husband.

Q: How will your life be similar/different from your mother's and grandmother's lives?

My mother's father walked out of her life when she was very young so she grew up with one parent. I've been lucky to have two. My mother didn't have much money even though my grandmother worked. My mother never went to college and I plan to. My mother does cashier work and some bookkeeping. If she had had my opportunities, she might have been an accountant.

Q: If you plan to marry, how do you see your partnership with a man?

First off, I'd like my marriage to be based on trust. As far as raising children, I guess all kids say this, that they won't raise their kids like their parents did, but I think I probably will. I want shared responsibilities, but my husband will probably have the final say concerning problems and decisions about the children, the house, the car, like in my parents' marriage. I think it will be this way for me because that's how I've seen it. That's the only way I know. I intend to go back to work when my kids are about five years old.

Q: What do you think is the biggest obstacle women face in achieving their goals?

Men. They're always putting us down. They say women are supposed to stay home and cook and take care of the kids. Women have a right to go out there and make their own careers and do whatever they want to do. I've heard men teachers say these things. Even my father, and my grandfather, too. And when they say it, I try to argue back and they usually end up winning the argument. When I say, "What right do you have to put us down?" they answer, "The male species is dominant and more powerful." I always say it's not fair and they shouldn't judge us just because we're women or girls, but they don't listen.

Q: What would you like women to achieve?

I don't really know.

Eighteen-year-old Esther Barela is a high school senior and lives in Zuni, New Mexico.

Q: Was there any time in your life that being a girl hindered you?

I remember when I was younger I had this impression that certain jobs were for men only and other jobs were for women only. As I entered junior high school, I began to realize then that more women were pursuing what they *wanted* to do, not what was expected of them. Sometimes I feel because of my traditions and how my mother and grandmother grew up, I'd have to follow what I was taught—a woman should stay home and be the keeper of the house and caretaker of the children. I [once] thought my choices were limited, but now I know they're not.

Q: What do you want to achieve in your life?

I hope to become a pediatrician. I am very interested in the health field because I see a great need for doctors in my community. [Esther Barela is a member of the Zuni Pueblo, a Native American community.] I have been told time and time again that no matter who I am or where I come from, I can do just about anything in life. I have set my goals really high because I know it's going to be a hard journey and the things I learn along the way will help me grow to become the best I can.

Q: How will your life be similar/different from your mother's and grandmother's lives?

I think my life will be different from theirs. My mother only graduated from high school. Then she went to a beauty school but she didn't finish because she had me. She never returned to school. Her work is usually as a clerk or cashier at a school. My grandmother didn't finish high school. She got married and lived on the reservation and brought up her kids there. Her life has been pretty confined to the reservation. I've probably gone more places in my eighteen years than my grandmother's gone in her sixty-four years.

My mother and grandmother take part in a lot of the traditional things of Zuni women. When we have traditional *kachina* dances, in which only the men dance, my mother and grandmother and the other women bake bread and cook foods. I don't do it. I don't know how to do it. I've asked my mother sometimes to teach me but I always seem too busy doing something else to learn.

I don't think I'm going to live on the reservation like they do. There are a lot of kids my age here who feel the same way. We have a hospital on the reservation. I might come back for my hospital residency but I'm not sure I'll stay.

Q: If you plan to marry, how do you see your partnership with a man?

I do plan to marry; not soon, but in time enough to get my life together and settle down. I want to make a stable life for myself so that if a relationship or marriage doesn't work out, I can depend on myself instead of my spouse. I want my relationship with my future husband to be one of trust, honesty, and respect. I want to be able to pursue my goals and not have him feel possessive or that he can't trust me. I'd want my husband to have his independence too. I realize that this kind of relationship may be hard to find but it's only a matter of waiting for that right person.

Q: What do you think is the biggest obstacle women face in achieving their goals? Are there any special obstacles you face being an American Indian?

I think the biggest obstacle women face in achieving their goals is themselves. If a person doesn't believe in herself or himself, then she or he can't really get anywhere. I really do stress that it doesn't matter where you come from or what sex, color, or age you are; if you have enough faith in yourself and what you hope to accomplish, the sky's the limit.

Q: What would you like women to achieve?

I would like women to achieve all they've ever dreamed of. I see this being done more and more and I want it to continue. I hope women realize that they are just as important in this world as men are. When it comes to achieving one's life goals, it matters not what gender, race, color or age one is, but how much determination and drive one possesses.

Notes

PART ONE Women in the New World

In the Beginning
Horatio Hale, "Huron Folk-Lore." *The Journal of American Folklore*, Vol. I, No. 3, Oct.–Dec. 1888, pp. 180–81.

Spooled a Piece
Sydney George Fisher, *Men, Women & Manners in Colonial Times*, p. 275. Philadelphia: Lippincott, 1898.

Pitty Your Destressed Daughter
Isabel M. Calder, ed., *Colonial Captivities, Marches and Journeys*, pp. 151–52. New York: Macmillan, 1935.

Always Leap Year
"Letter of Miss Rebecca Franks." *Pennsylvania Magazine of History and Biography*, Oct. 1899, pp. 303–9.

I Like This Part of the World
Eliza Lucas Pinckney, *Journals and Letters of Eliza Lucas*, pp. 6–7. Wormsloe, Ga., 1850.

If Ever Two Were One
John Harvard Ellis, ed., *The Works of Anne Bradstreet in Prose and Verse*, pp. 400–2 and 394. Boston: Abram E. Cutter, 1867.

Foul Words In My Ear
Linda Brent (Harriet Jacobs), "The Trials of Girlhood." *Incidents in the Life of a Slave Girl*, Lydia Maria Child, ed., pp. 44–45. Boston: Published for the author, 1861.

Fight, and If You Can't Fight, Kick
Ophelia Settle Egypt, J. Masouka, and Charles S. Johnson, *Unwritten History of Slavery: Autobiographical Accounts of Negro Ex-Slaves,* bound typescript pp. 284–91. Social Studies Source Documents No. 1. Nashville, Tenn.: Fisk University, Social Science Institute, 1945.

PART TWO The Question of Independence

Nor Fitting for Your Sex
Thomas Hutchinson, *The History of the Colony and Province of Massachusetts Bay*, Lawrence Shaw Mayo, ed., Vol. II, Appendix II, pp. 366–91. Cambridge: Harvard University Press, 1936.

Remember the Ladies
Charles Francis Adams, ed., *Familiar Letters of John Adams and His Wife Abigail Adams, During the Revolution,* pp. 148–49 and 155. Freeport, N.Y.: Books for Libraries Press, 1875.

I Would Not Go
"Diary of Grace Growden Galloway." *Pennsylvania Magazine,* Vol. 55, 1931–34, pp. 36–55.

Woman Is to Win Everything
Catharine E. Beecher, *An Essay on Slavery and Abolitionism, with Reference to the Duty of American Females,* pp. 98–100. Philadelphia: Henry Perkins, 1837.

Whatever Is *Right* for Man to Do

Sarah M. Grimké, *Letters on the Equality of the Sexes and the Condition of Women*, pp. 15–21. Boston: Isaac Knapp, 1838.

All Men and Women Are Created Equal

Elizabeth Cady Stanton, Susan B. Anthony, and Frances Gage, eds. *History of Woman Suffrage*, Vol. I, pp. 70–73. Rochester: Charles Mann, 1881.

And Ain't I a Woman?

Stanton, Anthony, and Gage, eds., *History of Woman Suffrage*, Vol. I., pp. 115–17.

While Acknowledging Our Mutual Affection . . .

Leslie Wheeler, ed., *Loving Warriors: Selected Letters of Lucy Stone and Henry Blackwell*, pp. 135–36. New York: Dial, 1981.

Our Arrival Set a Buzz Going

Stanton, Anthony, and Gage, eds., *History of Woman Suffrage*, Vol. II, pp. 234 and 238–42.

PART THREE Seeking an Education

Puddings and Seams

Judith Sargent Murray, "On the Equality of the Sexes." *The Massachusetts Magazine*, March 1790, pp. 132–34.

Promise Not to Tell

Susie King Taylor, *Reminiscences of My Life in Camp with the 33rd United States Colored Troops*, pp. 5–6. Boston: Published by the author, 1902.

Much Happiness
Antoinette Hubbell to Caroline E. Coles. Mount Holyoke Archives, South Hadley, Mass.

Works by the Piece
"Report of the Special Committee of the House on Labor," House Report No. 50, House 1–65, pp. 2–4. Boston: Massachusetts General Court Legislative Documents, 1845.

A Most Extraordinary Case
Dr. Elizabeth Blackwell, *Pioneer Work in Opening the Medical Profession to Women*, pp. 56–59, 154, 157–60. London: Everyman's Library, 1895.

All Sorts of Excuses
Alta, April 16, 1885, p. 1.

PART FOUR Settling the West

They Wept Silently
"An Indian Girl's Story of a Trading Expedition to the Southwest about 1841." *The Frontier*, May 1930, pp. 338–67.

Left Our Hitherto Happy Home
"A Journal of Mary Stuart Bailey." *Ho for California! Women's Overland Diaries from the Huntington Library*, Sandra L. Myres, ed., pp. 53–64. San Marino, Cal.: Huntington Library, 1980.

Four Walls and the Roof
Anna Howard Shaw, D.D., M.D., *The Story of a Pioneer*, pp. 20–33. New York: Harper, 1915.

There Was a Prejudice Against Female Teachers
Hartford, Conn.: Letters to the National Board of Popular Education Collection, Connecticut Historical Society.

Hogs in My Kitchen
Mary Ballou, *A Woman's View of the Gold Rush*. New Haven: Yale University Library, 1962.

In America There Was a Great Deal of Gold
Orientals and Their Cultural Adjustment, pp. 31–32. Social Science Source Documents No. 4. Nashville, Tenn.: Fisk University, Social Science Institute, 1946.

A Time Never to be Forgotten
Unpublished memoir of Ascension Sepulveda Mott, in possession of Choueta Lantz Earle.

PART FIVE Work and Politics

An Unfortunate Victim
Rosalyn Baxandall, Linda Gordon, and Susan Reverby, eds., *America's Working Women: A Documentary History*, pp. 120–21. New York: Random House, 1976.

And Learn of Life
Jane Addams, *Twenty Years at Hull-House*, pp. 64–71, 85–88. New York: Macmillan, 1915.

Nothing to Look Forward to
Barbara Wertheimer, *We Were There: The Story of Working Women in America*, pp. 294–95. New York: Pantheon, 1977.

This Is Not the First Time
Rose Schneiderman, *All for One*, p. 101. New York: P. S. Eriksson, 1967.

Is Peace More a Concern of Women?
Woman's Peace Party of New York City pamphlet, March 1918. Swarthmore, Pa.: Swarthmore College Peace Collection.

He Tore the Banner Down
Inez Haynes Irwin, *The Story of the Woman's Party*, pp. 230–275. New York: Harcourt, 1921.

PART SIX Race and Ethnicity

True Chivalry Respects All Womanhood
Ida Wells Barnett, *A Red Record*, pp. 8–15. Chicago: Donohue & Henneberry, 1895.

I Cannot Believe
Lyda B. Conley, "Huron Cemetery." Typed transcript taken from handwritten notes, 1909. Bonner Springs, Kan.: Wyandotte County Museum.

Outfitted with Western Clothing
Emma Gee, "Issei Women." *Asian Women* (Asian Women's Journal of the University of California at Berkeley), 1971, pp. 11–15.

A Girl Without a Cent
Rose Cohen, *Out of the Shadow*, pp. 204–26. New York: George H. Doran, 1918.

They Will Not Listen to Their Mother
William Thomas and Florian Znaniecki, *The Polish Peasant in Europe and America*, Eli Zaretsky, ed., pp. 150–54. Urbana, Ill.: University of Illinois Press, 1984.

PART SEVEN The Modern Woman

Dear Mrs. Sanger
Appeals from American Mothers, pp. 4–16. New York: Woman's Publishing Co., 1921.

Extraordinarily Free
Margaret Mead, *Blackberry Winter*, pp. 108–9; 164; 244–45; 248–54. New York: William Morrow & Company, 1972.

30 Cents an Hour
Louise Mitchell, "Slave Markets Typify Exploitation of Domestics." *The Daily Worker*, May 4, 1940. Second selection: Ellen Cantarow, Susan Gushell O'Malley, and Sharon Hartman Strom, *Moving the Mountain*, pp. 119–21. New York: Feminist Press, 1980.

Having Learned to Stare Down Fear
Eleanor Roosevelt, *The Autobiography of Eleanor Roosevelt*, pp. 411–12. New York: Harper, 1961.

Simply Remarkable
Jacqueline Cochran, typed transcript of an interview, pp. 34–44. Oral History Project, Columbia University.

You Should Be Home with the Children
Jennifer Colton, "Why I Quit Working." *Good Housekeeping*, Sept., 1951, pp. 53 and 177–79.

PART EIGHT The New Consciousness

The Problem That Has No Name
Betty Friedan, *The Feminine Mystique*, pp. 18–19, 43, 77–78. New York: Norton, 1963.

She Is Not Free Until I Am Free
Fannie Lou Hamer, speech given at NAACP Legal Defense Fund Institute, New York City, May 1971.

It's in Your Own Head
Barbara L. Maer and Glenna Matthews, "Women of the Boycott," *The Nation*, February 23, 1974, pp. 232–34.

What Got You Interested in the Woman's Movement?
Anne Koedt, Ellen Levine, and Anita Rapone, eds., *Radical Feminism*, pp. 280–81. New York: Quadrangle, 1973.

Why I Want a Wife
Koedt, Levine, and Rapone, eds., *Radical Feminism*, pp. 60–62.

The Gay Movement Helped Me Have a Family
This interview was conducted by the author in 1990.

I Just Couldn't Have Another Baby
Amicus brief in *Richard Thornburg v. American College of Obstetricians and Gynecologists, et al.*, U.S. No. 84-495 and 84-1379. October 1985.

Women Should Be Free
Barbara Peters and Victoria Samuels, eds., *Dialogue on Diversity: A New Agenda for American Women,* pp. 35–39. New York: American Jewish Committee Institute on Pluralism and Group Identity, 1976.

PART NINE What's Ahead?

These interviews were conducted in 1989–1990 by the author for the purposes of this book.

Bibliography

The starred* books are particularly appropriate for young adult readers.

General Histories

Flexner, Eleanor. *Century of Struggle*. New York: Atheneum, 1968.

*Kessler-Harris, Alice. *Women Have Always Worked*. Old Westbury, N.Y.: Feminist Press, 1981.

*McCunn, Ruthanne Lum. *Chinese American Portraits*. San Francisco: Chronicle Books, 1988.

Neithammer, Carolyn. *Daughters of the Earth: The Lives and Legends of American Indian Women*. New York: Macmillan, 1977.

Wertheimer, Barbara Meyer. *We Were There: The Story of Working Women in America*. New York: Pantheon, 1977.

Autobiographies, Biographies, and Letters

PART ONE Women in the New World

Bradford, Sarah, ed. *Harriet Tubman, The Moses of Her People.* New York: Corinth Books, 1961.

*Sterling, Dorothy. *Freedom Train: The Story of Harriet Tubman.* New York: Scholastic, 1954.

Lurie, Nancy Oestreich, ed. *Mountain Wolf Woman: The Autobiography of a Winnebago Woman.* Ann Arbor, Mich.: University of Michigan Press, 1961.

PART TWO The Question of Independence

Adams, Charles F., ed. *Familiar Letters of John Adams and His Wife Abigail Adams, During the Revolution.* New York: Books for Libraries Press, 1875.

Du Bois, Ellen Carol. *Elizabeth Cady Stanton/Susan B. Anthony. Correspondence, Writings, Speeches.* New York: Schocken, 1981.

Gilbert, Olive. *Narrative of Sojourner Truth.* New York: Published for the author, 1853.

*Reit, Seymour. *Behind Rebels Lines: The Incredible Story of Emma Edmonds, Civil War Spy.* New York: Gulliver Books, 1987.

Stanton, Elizabeth Cady. *Eighty Years More.* New York: Schocken, 1971.

Wheeler, Leslie, ed. *Loving Warriors: Selected Letters of Lucy Stone and Henry Blackwell.* New York: Dial, 1981.

PART THREE Seeking an Education

Blackwell, Elizabeth. *Pioneer Work in Opening the Medical Profession to Women.* London: Everyman's Library, 1895.

Hays, Elinor. *Those Extraordinary Blackwells.* New York: Harcourt, 1961.

*Larcom, Lucy. *A New England Girlhood.* Boston: Houghton Mifflin, 1889.

Taylor, Susie King. *Reminiscences of My Life in Camp with the 33rd United States Colored Troops.* Boston: Published by the author, 1902.

PART FOUR Settling the West

Owens-Adair, Bethenia. *Dr. Owens-Adair: Some of Her Life Experiences.* Portland, Ore.: Manor and Beach, 1904.

Schissel, Lillian, ed. *Women's Diaries of the Westward Journey.* New York: Schocken, 1982.

Shaw, Anna Howard. *The Story of a Pioneer.* New York: Harper, 1915.

Stewart, Elinor Pruitt. *Letters of a Woman Homesteader.* Lincoln, Neb.: University of Nebraska Press, 1961.

Winnemucca, Sarah Hopkins. *Life Among the Piutes, Their Wrongs and Doings.* Reprint, Bishop, Cal.: Chalfant Press, 1969.

PART FIVE Work and Politics

Addams, Jane. *Twenty Years at Hull-House.* New York: Macmillan, 1915.

Hamilton, Alice. *Exploring the Dangerous Trades.* Boston: Little, Brown, 1943.

Irwin, Inez Haynes. *The Story of the Woman's Party.* New York: Harcourt, 1921.

*Parton, Mary Field, ed. *The Autobiography of Mother Jones.* Chicago: Charles H. Kerr, 1925.

Wald, Lillian. *The House on Henry Street.* New York: Henry Holt, 1915.

PART SIX Race and Ethnicity

*Antin, Mary. *The Promised Land.* Boston: Houghton Mifflin, 1912.

*Cohen, Rose. *Out of the Shadows.* New York: George H. Doran, 1918.

*Duster, Alfred, ed. *Crusader for Justice: The Autobiography of Ida B. Wells.* Chicago: University of Chicago Press, 1970.

*Kingston, Maxine Hong. *The Woman Warrior.* New York: Knopf, 1976.

Wong, Jade Snow. *Fifth Chinese Daughter.* New York: Harper, 1965.

PART SEVEN The Modern Woman

Cochran, Jacqueline. *The Stars at Noon.* Boston: Little, Brown, 1954.

*Lauber, Patricia. *Lost Star: The Story of Amelia Earhart.* New York: Scholastic, 1988.

Mead, Margaret. *Blackberry Winter.* New York: Simon & Shuster, 1972.

*Patterson, Charles. *Marian Anderson.* New York: F. Watts, 1987.

Roosevelt, Eleanor. *This Is My Story.* New York: Harper, 1937.

Sanger, Margaret. *An Autobiography.* New York: Norton, 1938.

Schneiderman, Rose. *All for One.* New York: P. S. Eriksson, 1967.

PART EIGHT The New Consciousness

Cantarow, Ellen, Susan Gushell O'Malley, and Sharon Hartman Strom, eds. *Moving the Mountain: Women Working for Social Change.* Old Westbury, N.Y.: Feminist Press, 1980.

Friedan, Betty. *The Feminine Mystique.* New York: Norton, 1963.

Moody, Anne. *Coming of Age in Mississippi.* New York: Dial, 1968.

Index

Page numbers in *italics* refer to illustrations.

Knights of Labor, 152
Koedt, Anne, 259
Korean War, 225

labor shortage, 23, 209, 223
labor-union organizing, 96–98,
  151–55, 161–66, 176–77, 248–51,
  273. *See also* factory work, textile-
  mill work
Ladies Magazine, 50
lawsuits, feminism and, 253
lawyers, women. *See* legal profession
leadership, 38
Lee, Ellen, 131–34
legal profession, 63, 100, 154, 187,
  210, 277
legal status of women: blacks, 25,
  28–29, 90–91, 181–86, 218,
  244–45; in colonial times, 18–19,
  37–40; and contraception, 206,
  209; equal protection under the
  law, 58–73, 75, 252; factory
  workers, 160, 163, 166; free legal
  services, 152; and homesteading,
  125; married, 18–19, 42–49, 62,
  63, 71–73, 209;
  postrevolutionary America,
  42–49; and suffrage movement,
  173–76
Lemlich, Clara, 164
lesbians, 262–67, 271; and gay
  rights, 253
Lewis, Meriwether, and Clark,
  William, 111–12
Lewis, Mrs. (suffragist), 174, 175,
  176
Lincoln, President Abraham, 151
Little Rock High School, 244–45
Lockwood, Belva, 154

Louisiana Purchase, 111
Love, Nancy Harkness, 225
Lucas, Eliza, 16
"Lucy Stoners," 72–73
lynching, 182–86
Lyons, Mary, 92–93

McCall's, 273
McDonald, Catherine, 112–16
magazines, women's, 50, *51*, 209–10,
  230, 231–35, 239, 258
Marine Corps Women's Reserves
  (MCWR), 224–25
marriage: 99, 210, 280; arranged,
  191–97; in colonial times, 7,
  18–19, 20, 41–49; equality in, 59,
  62, 72–73, 259–62, 292; married
  women's legal status, 18–19,
  42–49, 62, 63, 71–73, 209; sharing domestic work, 278, 282–83,
  285, 286, 287; wedding ceremony,
  146–47
Massachusetts, 6, 20, 37–40, 54, 85,
  93, 94, 96, *97*, 97–99, 125, 151,
  152, 163
Massachusetts Bill of Rights, 28
maternity leave, paid, 252
Mead, Margaret, 210–14
medical care: availability of, 8, 208,
  211, 267–70; instituted by women,
  74, 155; women as care-givers, 8,
  37, 106, 118, 119; women doctors,
  63, 100–105, 154, 277, 291
medical profession, 63, 100–105,
  154, 210, 277, 291
medical school, 100–103, 154
Memphis, Tenn., 182, 183–84
men's work, 3–4, 8, 41, 50, 209
Mexican Americans, 6, 217, 219–20,